JUN .- '94

CH

MOTHER TERESA

Joan Graff Clucas

CHELSEA HOUSE PUBLISHERS
NEW YORK
PHILADELPHIA

EDITOR-IN-CHIEF: Nancy Toff
EXECUTIVE EDITOR: Remmel T. Nunn
MANAGING EDITOR: Karyn Gullen Browne
COPY CHIEF: Juliann Barbato
PICTURE EDITOR: Adrian G. Allen
ART DIRECTOR: Giannella Garrett
MANUFACTURING MANAGER: Gerald Levine

Staff for MOTHER TERESA:

SENIOR EDITOR: John W. Selfridge
ASSISTANT EDITOR: Kathleen McDermott
COPY EDITOR: Terrance Dolan
EDITORIAL ASSISTANT: Sean Ginty
ASSOCIATE PICTURE EDITOR: Juliette Dickstein
PICTURE RESEARCHER: Karen Herman
SENIOR DESIGNER: Debby Jay
ASSISTANT DESIGNER: Jill Goldreyer
PRODUCTION COORDINATOR: Joseph Romano
COVER ILLUSTRATION: David Dircks

CREATIVE DIRECTOR: Harold Steinberg

5 7 9 8 6 4

Library of Congress Cataloging in Publication Data

Clucas, Joan Graff.

Mother Teresa.

(World leaders past & present)
Bibliography: p.
Includes index.
Summary: A biography of the founder of the Missionary Sisters and
Brothers of Charity, known for her work with the destitute and dying in
Calcutta and other places and who was awarded the Nobel Peace Prize in
1979.
1. Teresa, Mother, 1910–   —Juvenile literature.
2. Missionaries of Charity—Biography—Juvenile literature.
[1. Teresa, Mother, 1910– . 2. Nuns. 3. Missionaries.
4. Missionaries of Charity—Biography. 5. Missions—India]
I. Title. II. Series.
BX4406.5.Z8C58   1988   271'.97 [B] [92]   87-26829
ISBN 1-55546-855-1
      0-7910-0602-6 (pbk.)

Contents

WORLD LEADERS   PAST & PRESENT

JOHN ADAMS
JOHN QUINCY ADAMS
KONRAD ADENAUER
ALEXANDER THE GREAT
SALVADOR ALLENDE
MARC ANTONY
CORAZON AQUINO
YASIR ARAFAT
KING ARTHUR
HAFEZ AL-ASSAD
KEMAL ATATÜRK
ATTILA
CLEMENT ATTLEE
AUGUSTUS CAESAR
MENACHEM BEGIN
DAVID BEN-GURION
OTTO VON BISMARCK
LÉON BLUM
SIMON BOLÍVAR
CESARE BORGIA
WILLY BRANDT
LEONID BREZHNEV
JULIUS CAESAR
JOHN CALVIN
JIMMY CARTER
FIDEL CASTRO
CATHERINE THE GREAT
CHARLEMAGNE
CHIANG KAI-SHEK
WINSTON CHURCHILL
GEORGES CLEMENCEAU
CLEOPATRA
CONSTANTINE THE GREAT
HERNÁN CORTÉS
OLIVER CROMWELL
GEORGES-JACQUES
    DANTON
JEFFERSON DAVIS
MOSHE DAYAN
CHARLES DE GAULLE
EAMON DE VALERA
EUGENE DEBS
DENG XIAOPING
BENJAMIN DISRAELI
ALEXANDER DUBČEK
FRANÇOIS & JEAN-CLAUDE
    DUVALIER
DWIGHT EISENHOWER
ELEANOR OF AQUITAINE
ELIZABETH I
FAISAL
FERDINAND & ISABELLA
FRANCISCO FRANCO
BENJAMIN FRANKLIN

FREDERICK THE GREAT
INDIRA GANDHI
MOHANDAS GANDHI
GIUSEPPE GARIBALDI
AMIN & BASHIR GEMAYEL
GENGHIS KHAN
WILLIAM GLADSTONE
MIKHAIL GORBACHEV
ULYSSES S. GRANT
ERNESTO "CHE" GUEVARA
TENZIN GYATSO
ALEXANDER HAMILTON
DAG HAMMARSKJÖLD
HENRY VIII
HENRY OF NAVARRE
PAUL VON HINDENBURG
HIROHITO
ADOLF HITLER
HO CHI MINH
KING HUSSEIN
IVAN THE TERRIBLE
ANDREW JACKSON
JAMES I
WOJCIECH JARUZELSKI
THOMAS JEFFERSON
JOAN OF ARC
POPE JOHN XXIII
POPE JOHN PAUL II
LYNDON JOHNSON
BENITO JUÁREZ
JOHN KENNEDY
ROBERT KENNEDY
JOMO KENYATTA
AYATOLLAH KHOMEINI
NIKITA KHRUSHCHEV
KIM IL SUNG
MARTIN LUTHER KING, JR.
HENRY KISSINGER
KUBLAI KHAN
LAFAYETTE
ROBERT E. LEE
VLADIMIR LENIN
ABRAHAM LINCOLN
DAVID LLOYD GEORGE
LOUIS XIV
MARTIN LUTHER
JUDAS MACCABEUS
JAMES MADISON
NELSON & WINNIE
    MANDELA
MAO ZEDONG
FERDINAND MARCOS
GEORGE MARSHALL

MARY, QUEEN OF SCOTS
TOMÁŠ MASARYK
GOLDA MEIR
KLEMENS VON METTERNICH
JAMES MONROE
HOSNI MUBARAK
ROBERT MUGABE
BENITO MUSSOLINI
NAPOLÉON BONAPARTE
GAMAL ABDEL NASSER
JAWAHARLAL NEHRU
NERO
NICHOLAS II
RICHARD NIXON
KWAME NKRUMAH
DANIEL ORTEGA
MOHAMMED REZA PAHLAVI
THOMAS PAINE
CHARLES STEWART
    PARNELL
PERICLES
JUAN PERÓN
PETER THE GREAT
POL POT
MUAMMAR EL-QADDAFI
RONALD REAGAN
CARDINAL RICHELIEU
MAXIMILIEN ROBESPIERRE
ELEANOR ROOSEVELT
FRANKLIN ROOSEVELT
THEODORE ROOSEVELT
ANWAR SADAT
HAILE SELASSIE
PRINCE SIHANOUK
JAN SMUTS
JOSEPH STALIN
SUKARNO
SUN YAT-SEN
TAMERLANE
MOTHER TERESA
MARGARET THATCHER
JOSIP BROZ TITO
TOUSSAINT L'OUVERTURE
LEON TROTSKY
PIERRE TRUDEAU
HARRY TRUMAN
QUEEN VICTORIA
LECH WALESA
GEORGE WASHINGTON
CHAIM WEIZMANN
WOODROW WILSON
XERXES
EMILIANO ZAPATA
ZHOU ENLAI

CHELSEA HOUSE PUBLISHERS

ON LEADERSHIP

Arthur M. Schlesinger, jr.

LEADERSHIP, it may be said, is really what makes the world go round. Love no doubt smooths the passage; but love is a private transaction between consenting adults. Leadership is a public transaction with history. The idea of leadership affirms the capacity of individuals to move, inspire, and mobilize masses of people so that they act together in pursuit of an end. Sometimes leadership serves good purposes, sometimes bad; but whether the end is benign or evil, great leaders are those men and women who leave their personal stamp on history.

Now, the very concept of leadership implies the proposition that individuals can make a difference. This proposition has never been universally accepted. From classical times to the present day, eminent thinkers have regarded individuals as no more than the agents and pawns of larger forces, whether the gods and goddesses of the ancient world or, in the modern era, race, class, nation, the dialectic, the will of the people, the spirit of the times, history itself. Against such forces, the individual dwindles into insignificance.

So contends the thesis of historical determinism. Tolstoy's great novel *War and Peace* offers a famous statement of the case. Why, Tolstoy asked, did millions of men in the Napoleonic Wars, denying their human feelings and their common sense, move back and forth across Europe slaughtering their fellows? "The war," Tolstoy answered, "was bound to happen simply because it was bound to happen." All prior history predetermined it. As for leaders, they, Tolstoy said, "are but the labels that serve to give a name to an end and, like labels, they have the least possible connection with the event." The greater the leader, "the more conspicuous the inevitability and the predestination of every act he commits." The leader, said Tolstoy, is "the slave of history."

Determinism takes many forms. Marxism is the determinism of class. Nazism the determinism of race. But the idea of men and women as the slaves of history runs athwart the deepest human instincts. Rigid determinism abolishes the idea of human freedom—

the assumption of free choice that underlies every move we make, every word we speak, every thought we think. It abolishes the idea of human responsibility, since it is manifestly unfair to reward or punish people for actions that are by definition beyond their control. No one can live consistently by any deterministic creed. The Marxist states prove this themselves by their extreme susceptibility to the cult of leadership.

More than that, history refutes the idea that individuals make no difference. In December 1931 a British politician crossing Park Avenue in New York City between 76th and 77th Streets around 10:30 P.M. looked in the wrong direction and was knocked down by an automobile—a moment, he later recalled, of a man aghast, a world aglare: "I do not understand why I was not broken like an eggshell or squashed like a gooseberry." Fourteen months later an American politician, sitting in an open car in Miami, Florida, was fired on by an assassin; the man beside him was hit. Those who believe that individuals make no difference to history might well ponder whether the next two decades would have been the same had Mario Constasino's car killed Winston Churchill in 1931 and Giuseppe Zangara's bullet killed Franklin Roosevelt in 1933. Suppose, in addition, that Adolf Hitler had been killed in the street fighting during the Munich *Putsch* of 1923 and that Lenin had died of typhus during World War I. What would the 20th century be like now?

For better or for worse, individuals do make a difference. "The notion that a people can run itself and its affairs anonymously," wrote the philosopher William James, "is now well known to be the silliest of absurdities. Mankind does nothing save through initiatives on the part of inventors, great or small, and imitation by the rest of us—these are the sole factors in human progress. Individuals of genius show the way, and set the patterns, which common people then adopt and follow."

Leadership, James suggests, means leadership in thought as well as in action. In the long run, leaders in thought may well make the greater difference to the world. But, as Woodrow Wilson once said, "Those only are leaders of men, in the general eye, who lead in action. . . . It is at their hands that new thought gets its translation into the crude language of deeds." Leaders in thought often invent in solitude and obscurity, leaving to later generations the tasks of imitation. Leaders in action—the leaders portrayed in this series—have to be effective in their own time.

And they cannot be effective by themselves. They must act in response to the rhythms of their age. Their genius must be adapted, in a phrase of William James's, "to the receptivities of the moment." Leaders are useless without followers. "There goes the mob," said the French politician hearing a clamor in the streets. "I am their leader. I must follow them." Great leaders turn the inchoate emotions of the mob to purposes of their own. They seize on the opportunities of their time, the hopes, fears, frustrations, crises, potentialities. They succeed when events have prepared the way for them, when the community is awaiting to be aroused, when they can provide the clarifying and organizing ideas. Leadership ignites the circuit between the individual and the mass and thereby alters history.

It may alter history for better or for worse. Leaders have been responsible for the most extravagant follies and most monstrous crimes that have beset suffering humanity. They have also been vital in such gains as humanity has made in individual freedom, religious and racial tolerance, social justice, and respect for human rights.

There is no sure way to tell in advance who is going to lead for good and who for evil. But a glance at the gallery of men and women in *World Leaders—Past and Present* suggests some useful tests.

One test is this: Do leaders lead by force or by persuasion? By command or by consent? Through most of history leadership was exercised by the divine right of authority. The duty of followers was to defer and to obey. "Theirs not to reason why / Theirs but to do and die." On occasion, as with the so-called enlightened despots of the 18th century in Europe, absolutist leadership was animated by humane purposes. More often, absolutism nourished the passion for domination, land, gold, and conquest and resulted in tyranny.

The great revolution of modern times has been the revolution of equality. The idea that all people should be equal in their legal condition has undermined the old structure of authority, hierarchy, and deference. The revolution of equality has had two contrary effects on the nature of leadership. For equality, as Alexis de Tocqueville pointed out in his great study *Democracy in America*, might mean equality in servitude as well as equality in freedom.

"I know of only two methods of establishing equality in the political world," Tocqueville wrote. "Rights must be given to every citizen, or none at all to anyone . . . save one, who is the master of all." There was no middle ground "between the sovereignty of all and the absolute power of one man." In his astonishing prediction of 20th-century totalitarian dictatorship, Tocqueville explained how the revolution of equality could lead to the *"Führerprinzip"* and more terrible absolutism than the world had ever known.

But when rights are given to every citizen and the sovereignty of all is established, the problem of leadership takes a new form, becomes more exacting than ever before. It is easy to issue commands and enforce them by the rope and the stake, the concentration camp and the *gulag*. It is much harder to use argument and achievement to overcome opposition and win consent. The Founding Fathers of the United States understood the difficulty. They believed that history had given them the opportunity to decide, as Alexander Hamilton wrote in the first Federalist Paper, whether men are indeed capable of basing government on "reflection and choice, or whether they are forever destined to depend . . . on accident and force."

Government by reflection and choice called for a new style of leadership and a new quality of followership. It required leaders to be responsive to popular concerns, and it required followers to be active and informed participants in the process. Democracy does not eliminate emotion from politics; sometimes it fosters demagoguery; but it is confident that, as the greatest of democratic leaders put it, you cannot fool all of the people all of the time. It measures leadership by results and retires those who overreach or falter or fail.

It is true that in the long run despots are measured by results too. But they can postpone the day of judgment, sometimes indefinitely, and in the meantime they can do infinite harm. It is also true that democracy is no guarantee of virtue and intelligence in government, for the voice of the people is not necessarily the voice of God. But democracy, by assuring the right of opposition, offers built-in resistance to the evils inherent in absolutism. As the theologian Reinhold Niebuhr summed it up, "Man's capacity for justice makes democracy possible, but man's inclination to injustice makes democracy necessary."

A second test for leadership is the end for which power is sought. When leaders have as their goal the supremacy of a master race or the promotion of totalitarian revolution or the acquisition and exploitation of colonies or the protection of greed and privilege or the preservation of personal power, it is likely that their leadership will do little to advance the cause of humanity. When their goal is the abolition of slavery, the liberation of women, the enlargement of opportunity for the poor and powerless, the extension of equal rights to racial minorities, the defense of the freedoms of expression and opposition, it is likely that their leadership will increase the sum of human liberty and welfare.

Leaders have done great harm to the world. They have also conferred great benefits. You will find both sorts in this series. Even "good" leaders must be regarded with a certain wariness. Leaders are not demigods; they put on their trousers one leg after another just like ordinary mortals. No leader is infallible, and every leader needs to be reminded of this at regular intervals. Irreverence irritates leaders but is their salvation. Unquestioning submission corrupts leaders and demeans followers. Making a cult of a leader is always a mistake. Fortunately hero worship generates its own antidote. "Every hero," said Emerson, "becomes a bore at last."

The signal benefit the great leaders confer is to embolden the rest of us to live according to our own best selves, to be active, insistent, and resolute in affirming our own sense of things. For great leaders attest to the reality of human freedom against the supposed inevitabilities of history. And they attest to the wisdom and power that may lie within the most unlikely of us, which is why Abraham Lincoln remains the supreme example of great leadership. A great leader, said Emerson, exhibits new possibilities to all humanity. "We feed on genius. . . . Great men exist that there may be greater men."

Great leaders, in short, justify themselves by emancipating and empowering their followers. So humanity struggles to master its destiny, remembering with Alexis de Tocqueville: "It is true that around every man a fatal circle is traced beyond which he cannot pass; but within the wide verge of that circle he is powerful and free; as it is with man, so with communities."

1

Love in Action

In the summer of 1982, tensions in the steaming caldron of the Middle East reached the boiling point as Israeli troops streamed across their northern border into Lebanon. The purpose of the Israeli invasion was to wipe out the Palestine Liberation Organization (PLO), which had set up bases in Lebanon. The PLO, an organization dedicated to the overthrow of the state of Israel and the recovery of the land it felt had been taken illegally from the Arab Palestinian people, was using the bases to launch raids and attacks on the neighboring Jewish state. Although the Israeli invasion was a well-executed military victory, many people disagreed with the move. For in the wake of the Israeli attack, violence erupted among many groups: between Israelis and Palestinians, Muslims and Christians; between weary soldiers and hostile civilians. Some people were just caught in the passions aroused by the fighting; some were the innocent victims of deliberate massacre. Before the attack was over, the Lebanese people suffered immeasurably, with a loss of life that amounted to almost 20,000 people. The number of wounded reached 30,000.

In a plain white room inside a school building in Beirut, Mother Teresa, an Albanian Catholic nun from Calcutta, India, and Catholic church officials

What stunned everyone was her energy. She saw the problem, fell to her knees, and prayed for a few seconds, and then she was rattling off a list of supplies she needed. . . . We didn't expect a saint to be so efficient.
—Red Cross official
on Mother Teresa's
work in Beirut

Mother Teresa embraces a frightened boy in a Palestinian refugee camp in Lebanon. Upon arriving in the war-torn country in 1982, she was overwhelmed by the suffering she saw and rushed to help, giving little regard for her own safety.

A smiling Mother Teresa greets students outside the Missionaries of Charity school in East Beirut. The school was established in 1979 to provide free education for the children of families impoverished by civil war in Lebanon.

from Christ the King Church and Mission Hospital in Juniyah, Lebanon, were discussing the grim situation: In addition to the misery of the Israeli invasion, a civil war had been raging between Muslims and Christians in that tiny Mediterranean country since 1975.

"This is not just an idea," Mother Teresa quietly asserted. "It is our duty." Lines of experience and care etched her sun-browned face. It was a face filled with kindness and determination. Mother Teresa was proposing crossing the battle zone between Muslim West and Christian East Beirut — called the Green Line — in order to rescue a group of abandoned children.

Mother Teresa, at 72, had been urged to stay away from Lebanon, a Middle East hot spot where the sky was continuously darkened by the smoke of explosions as vicious battles raged almost daily. However, she insisted on visiting the Missionaries of Charity school that she and her order had founded in the Armenian section of East Beirut. They had established the school in 1979 to provide services for families robbed of homes and possessions by the ravages of the civil war.

Although she had been encouraged to go to Egypt until the conflict lessened, she had taken a 17-hour ferry ride — intense fighting surrounding the Beirut airport prevented taking a plane — in sweltering heat from the island of Cyprus to Lebanon. After arriving in Lebanon, she still had an hour-long wait before she was escorted by Christian militiamen to a customs room.

From there, Mother Teresa and an American colleague, Ann Petrie, went to their destination, the Al-Rabih School in East Beirut. Seven nuns and 15 children greeted her. Mother Teresa sat in a schoolroom and faced two Catholic church officials who served in Beirut. She spoke to them of her plan to cross into West Beirut. That West Beirut was con-

Prasad Agarval, India's ambassador to Lebanon, confers with Mother Teresa during a visit to the Missionaries of Charity school in Beirut. Albanian by birth, Mother Teresa became an Indian citizen in 1949.

trolled by Muslims did not matter to her. "I feel the Church should be there *now*," she said quietly. "We don't mix up with politics and we must be there." Her expression remained determined.

She met a wall of resistance. The church officials insisted the time was wrong and told her that she should wait until the heavy shelling ended. One of the fathers brought up the possibility of being trapped on the west side if they went over by car. He then informed her that several priests had been killed recently in Beirut, seemingly just for the sake of killing.

Mother Teresa was undeterred. After all, she had risked her life every time she had picked up each of the 42,000 diseased and dying people she had rescued from the streets of Calcutta. If she had never risked touching the first one, her work would have died. She resolutely went on with her own battle plan, describing how individuals could be picked up one by one and brought over to the east. She was willing to go herself to implore the military personnel on both sides to help in the rescue effort.

The next day, Mother Teresa asked to see Philip Habib, the U.S. special envoy to the Middle East, in the hope that he might help. He reiterated the priests' concerns, asking, "Mother, do you hear the shells? It's absolutely impossible for you to cross at this time." He carefully described the danger and told her of the necessity of a cease-fire before anything could be done. She replied, "I have been praying to our Lady and I have asked her to let us have a cease-fire here tomorrow, the day before her feast day." Mr. Habib was skeptical that a cease-fire could be arranged so quickly, but he told Mother Teresa, "I believe in prayer . . . and I am a man of faith. . . . If we have the cease-fire, I personally will make arrangements for you to go to West Beirut tomorrow."

A cease-fire agreement went into effect the following day. Whether or not Mother Teresa's prayer had been answered, her strength of purpose and extraordinary sense of fairness impressed the military leaders in Lebanon. During the cease-fire, in response to her question about where help was most

> *Today, nations put too much effort and money into defending their borders. If they could only defend defenseless people with food, shelter, and clothing, I think the world would be a happier place.*
> —MOTHER TERESA

Philip Habib briefs reporters on the latest developments in the Mideast. As the U.S. special envoy to the region during Mother Teresa's 1982 visit, Habib assisted in her evacuation of 37 mentally ill children from West Beirut.

needed, John de Salis, a Red Cross official, explained the plight of 37 mentally ill children who had been left in a hospital that had been shelled. Explosives had blown out windows, punched holes in walls, and blasted apart the top two floors. The hospital was practically evacuated. With no electricity, little water, limited supplies, and the very real chance that they would be killed by bombardment, the children's future there looked bleak. No one had yet volunteered to take these children, so Mother Teresa agreed to rescue them.

Accompanied by International Red Cross workers, Mother Teresa arrived at the hospital. She met with the few remaining staff members, who told her that 10 people had been killed, and dozens of others wounded, including some of the children. Under the able and active direction of Mother Teresa, the Red Cross volunteers and the hospital employees began their lifesaving work. The children, ranging in age from 7 to 21, sat in huddled groups on the floor. Many of them could not comprehend what had befallen them and wept from confusion and fear. Dr. Abdel Rahman Labban, chief medical officer, welcomed the actions of Mother Teresa to help these forgotten children. He observed, "You don't need intelligence to have fear. They cannot analyze it or even talk to others about it. But emotions don't need intelligence."

Mother Teresa walked among them, patting a head, holding a hand, and generally giving comfort. Wasting no time, she picked up the first child to be transported. One by one, the frightened children were carried to four waiting Red Cross vehicles. Cries, moans, and sobs broke the stillness of the cease-fire as the rapid evacuation was completed.

The procession of cars sped back across the dirt and rubble-filled streets. Familiar Red Cross flags waved from each one while the plaintive sirens wailed. The confused and terrified children stared from the windows as they crossed the Green Line into the safety of East Beirut. Soon all the children were resting in cleaner, more secure surroundings.

A horse-drawn cart passes strollers and bicyclists as it makes its way down the main street of a Macedonian village not far from Skopje, the birthplace of Agnes Bojaxhiu. The future Mother Teresa was born in 1910 to an Albanian merchant family.

Dressings and bandages were changed by the Missionaries of Charity sisters while the volunteers' soothing voices and capable hands put the children at ease.

Mother Teresa labored along with the sisters. She crooned to a severely emaciated child and asked one of the Lebanese sisters about obtaining a soybean formula for malnutrition. Caressing a crying child until he relaxed, she flashed her infectious smile. She had learned to maintain a cheerful spirit in the face of adversity.

Mother Teresa was accustomed to seeing hunger and disease. She had long worked to aid victims of poverty and natural catastrophes, but this was the first time she had witnessed the devastation of war, when human beings purposefully inflicted harm on one another. In a mournful tone she said, "I have never been in a war before, but I have seen famine and death. I was asking myself what do they feel when they do this? I don't understand it. They are all children of God. Why do they do it? I don't understand."

The story of Mother Teresa's childhood and youth is, quite simply, a demonstration of how God can take the life of any individual who is willing to offer it to him, and make of it something quite literally superhuman in its power and effectiveness.
—DAVID PORTER
British author

On August 27, 1910, Drana and Nikola (Kole) Bojaxhiu had their third and last child, a girl they named Agnes Gonxha. Agnes was born in Skopje, a tiny town in Macedonia, a region in the middle of the Balkan Peninsula, located to the east of Italy across the Adriatic Sea. At the time of Agnes's birth, the Balkans contained a unique blend of many different peoples who were antagonistic not only to the ruling powers but also, frequently, to each other. The numbers of different ethnic and linguistic groups, including Greek, Albanian, Turkish, Serbian, Bulgarian, and Macedonian, each with its own aspirations for independence and national integrity, earned the politically and socially volatile peninsula a reputation as the "powder keg of Europe."

Agnes's parents were Albanians who had settled in Macedonia, which at that time was part of the Ottoman Empire. Nikola Bojaxhiu was a popular merchant with a keen interest in politics. He was a member of the Skopje town council and was also involved in an underground organization that sought to gain Albanian independence from the Ottoman Turks. By the early 20th century, the Ottoman Turks had been a power in the Balkans for 500 years. The Ottoman Empire, plagued by widespread corruption, was in the last stages of decay, and the desperate Turks ruled their remaining territories with an iron hand.

Agnes Bojaxhiu grew up under the threat of war. The year of her birth saw the first Albanian uprising against the land's Turkish masters. When she was two, the First Balkan War broke out, in which Bulgaria, Greece, Montenegro, and Serbia defeated the Ottomans, stripping the Turks of most of their territory in Europe. Macedonia was divided among them, and Skopje came under the rule of Serbia. Although Albania achieved its longed-for independence in 1912, Kole Bojaxhiu continued his nationalist work by joining a movement dedicated to the incorporation of the Serbian region of Kosovo — inhabited largely by Albanians — into the new Albanian nation.

Kole Bojaxhiu enjoyed the life of a relatively prosperous merchant. He owned several houses and became the partner of an Italian merchant. He often traveled throughout Europe buying and selling

A Bulgarian soldier gives water to his enemy, a wounded Turk, during the First Balkan War. This 1912 conflict broke out in Agnes Bojaxhiu's homeland when several Balkan states rose up against the Ottoman Empire, which had ruled the Balkans for 500 years.

goods. When he returned to his family, he always brought presents for his children: his older daughter, Aga, his son, Lazar, and young Agnes. Although rather strict in matters of discipline, Kole was a loving and progressive father, even promoting the education of his daughters, an uncommon attitude in that era.

The Bojaxhius were part of the region's Catholic minority, and Kole and Drana Bojaxhiu were deeply religious. Kole gave generous contributions to the local parish church, and the Bojaxhius never turned away anyone in need. Kole was known locally for donating food and providing shelter to those in distress. He once told Agnes, "My daughter, never take a morsel of food that you are not prepared to share with others."

In June 1914 the Balkan powder keg finally exploded when a Serbian nationalist assassinated Franz Ferdinand, the archduke of Austria, and World War I began. One victim of the ensuing political chaos may have been Nikola Bojaxhiu. In 1918, at a meeting of Albanian nationalists in Belgrade, he was suddenly taken violently ill. Brought to Skopje by carriage, he underwent emergency surgery but died the following day. His family was convinced that he had been poisoned by political opponents. The residents of Skopje greatly mourned the loss of their friend and patron. His death was a devastating blow to his family. During his lifetime, Kole had been the family's sole means of support. Drana was now left with three young children and no income.

To support her family, Drana, a fine seamstress, became a dressmaker. Despite her hard life, she found the time to lend a hand helping the local poor. This spirit of generosity was perhaps her greatest influence on her children. Even as a young girl, Agnes began to accompany her mother on her visits to the sick, the elderly, and the lonely. From an early age, Agnes exhibited a tenderness for those less fortunate than she.

When she was not working or taking care of her children, Drana Bojaxhiu spent her time at the

In June 1914 World War I erupted soon after a Serbian nationalist assassinated Austrian archduke Franz Ferdinand. Nikola Bojaxhiu, Agnes's father, was a member of one of the many nationalist groups that thrived in central and eastern Europe.

Church of the Sacred Heart in Skopje, organizing prayer groups and arranging special observances. Every year the family made a pilgrimage to nearby Montenegro, where they, along with hundreds of others, worshiped the Madonna of Letnice. The annual pilgrimages, when the family was all together, were particularly happy times for Agnes.

At times Drana Bojaxhiu worried about her youngest daughter, who was rather frail and subject to coughs. When Agnes was not accompanying her mother on her visits, she lost herself in books, and she displayed a fondness for contemplation and solitude unusual in a child. Agnes enjoyed saying her prayers on her own and often could be found kneeling in church when no one else was there. Agnes became imbued with her mother's personal faith and desire to serve God in a practical, helpful way. She also took from Drana the belief that doing the Lord's work was reward enough in itself; recognition for it was not necessary or desirable. Drana Bojaxhiu told her children, "When you do good, do it unobtrusively, as if you were tossing a pebble into the sea." Her mother's strong, kind spirit made a lasting impression on Agnes.

Drana Bojaxhiu patiently taught her children about sacrifice and integrity. Once, when a wealthy woman came to the Bojaxhiu home to order a dress and proceeded to speak uncharitably about someone, Mrs. Bojaxhiu interrupted her and pointed to a plaque positioned over the door of the front room. It read: In this house, no one must speak against another. Indignant at being scolded by a poor seamstress, the woman picked up her belongings and walked out. Although her family certainly could have used the money from the job, Drana Bojaxhiu said to her children, "We can do without money, but we cannot do with sin. Let hundreds go, but I will not allow any impurity into my heart."

The three Bojaxhiu children were very close. Aga, though five years older than Agnes, had much in common with her. Both enjoyed reading and schoolwork. Aga was a somewhat better student than Agnes, but they were equal in their singing ability

As a schoolgirl, Agnes, as she was then called, was caught in the wave of enthusiasm for the missions and for the expansion of the Kingdom of Christ, a truly spiritual Kingdom.
—JULIEN HENRY
Jesuit priest and longtime friend of Mother Teresa

The spires of St. Stephen's Cathedral in Zagreb, Croatia, bear witness to a strong Catholic presence in northwest Yugoslavia. In the southern part of the country, however, Catholicism was an unpopular religion embraced mostly by members of the Albanian minority, including the Bojaxhius.

Western missionaries and their Indian students gather for a group portrait. Young Agnes Bojaxhiu heard reports at her local church about missionary work. They stirred her imagination, and she decided to become a missionary herself.

in the local choir. Both had unusually fine voices; Agnes's clear soprano rang with her devotion. She also poured forth her faith in poems; she is reported to have been a talented writer, although none of her efforts has survived. At the local government school Agnes attended, she gladly helped out her classmates with work. She thought of becoming a teacher, for she loved working with young children.

By the time she was 12, Agnes was convinced that her true vocation was the religious life. In 1924, the new parish priest, a Jesuit named Father Jambrenkovic, arrived, and he soon established a branch of the Sodality of the Blessed Virgin Mary, a church society for young girls. Agnes immediately joined. Drana was aware of her daughter's passion for the church; she did not actively encourage or discourage Agnes but merely waited to see whether it was a passing phase or a true calling.

One evening Father Jambrenkovic called a special meeting to tell his new congregation about Catholic missionaries who traveled around the world helping the poor and spreading the faith. Agnes eagerly gazed at the huge world map he had set up for the meeting and surprised the congregation by confidently pointing out the locations of various Catholic

This 1928 photograph shows Agnes as a pensive 18 year old. Her early interest in the church had by then grown into a passionate determination to dedicate her life to serving God.

missions. She had already read about such work in Catholic magazines and had been thrilled by the letters from Croatian missionaries in India that the priest read aloud during church services. She had found out all she could about mission work. A seed had been planted in the 14-year-old girl. She began to think that not only would she become a nun, but that she would join an order of missionaries.

During her senior year of high school, she began seriously to consider the possibility of a life dedicated to God. Through the church she learned of the Loreto order, a group of nuns who worked in Bengal, India. As Agnes prayed for guidance, she believed she felt God's call to go to the missions in India, and she decided to answer the call. She realized that to join the order would mean abandoning the comforts of her home; she would be separated from her family, perhaps forever. But the determined young woman never looked back. As she later said, "I decided to leave my home and become a nun, and since then I've never doubted that I've done the right thing. It was the will of God. It was his choice."

2

Loreto

At the age of 18, Agnes Bojaxhiu's solitary vision was to join the Loreto order, a group of nuns who worked in India. Her resolution came as no surprise to her parish priest, Father Jambrenkovic, but it was quite a shock to her family. According to Mother Teresa, upon hearing of her daughter's decision, Drana Bojaxhiu went to her room, closed the door, and remained there for 24 hours. Undoubtedly her daughter's decision caused Drana deep heartache, but as a religious woman, she acquiesced and told Agnes, "Put your hand in his and walk all the way with him."

Agnes's brother and sister each took the news differently. Aga Bojaxhiu loved her younger sister and was saddened by the thought of her leaving, but felt it would be best for Agnes to follow her heart. Lazar Bojaxhiu, now a soldier in the army of Albania's king Zog, read of Agnes's plan in a letter she sent him. He reacted with disbelief and frustration and told Agnes that she would be burying herself, wasting her life. Agnes replied with a strong letter of her own. "Lazar," she wrote, "you feel you are important as an official, serving a king of two million people. I am an official too, serving the king of the whole world."

Aware that the time of her departure was fast ap-

In Loreto I was the happiest nun in the world.
—MOTHER TERESA
on her early life with the
Loreto order

An emaciated man eats a simple meal on the streets of Calcutta, India. Moved by stories of missionaries who alleviated the miseries of the poor, 18-year-old Agnes Bojaxhiu left her family and friends to join the Loreto order, a group of missionary nuns who worked in India.

Ahmed Bey Zogu was president of the Albanian Republic when he posed for this formal portrait in 1927, the year before he was proclaimed King Zog I. Agnes's brother, Lazar, served in Zog's army.

proaching, Agnes was determined to store up memories of her home country. She took a last walk along the beautiful Vardar River, watched the sheep graze on the rolling hills, and enjoyed a final visit with friends at church. Her friends, sorry to see her leave, arranged a concert in her honor. Some brought gifts, and all carried good wishes for her future.

Finally, it was time for Agnes to travel to the Loreto Abbey in Dublin, Ireland, where she was to study English. On September 25, 1928, Agnes rode with Drana and Aga Bojaxhiu from Skopje north to Zagreb, in Croatia, where she would board another train to complete the next leg of her journey. Weeping, she waved a final good-bye to her beloved mother and sister.

Another young woman bound for the Loreto Abbey, Betike Kanjc, joined Agnes on the train at Zagreb. After many tiring days of travel, they stopped in Paris, France, where they were received by the mother superior of the local Loreto order. They then traveled on to Ireland, finally arriving at the capital, where they were taken to the Loreto Abbey at Rathfarnham. The convent was a simple structure built of red brick and accented with white, wooden window casements. The convent stood behind an imposing barred gate, but in the courtyard stood a statue of the Virgin Mary with open arms, as if to say, "Welcome home."

Agnes was at the convent for one reason: to learn English, the language the nuns used to teach India's schoolchildren. She tried to ignore the strange surroundings and concentrated on learning the language she needed. Dressed in the long white habit and black veil of the Loreto nuns, Agnes spent her days studying with Mother M. Borgia Irwin. Six weeks later, it was decided that Agnes and Betike knew enough English to travel to India, where they would spend their novitiate — the period of study

Agnes (standing) poses with her sister, Aga (seated, left), and a family friend in 1928, the year she left Skopje. In September, Aga accompanied Agnes to the train station in Zagreb to say goodbye. It was the last time the sisters saw each other.

and contemplation a nun undergoes before taking her vows.

In November 1928 Agnes and Betike started out for India. They were on a ship for seven weeks, sailing through the Suez Canal, down the Red Sea, and across the Indian Ocean, which was the most direct route between Europe and India. There was no Catholic priest on the ship, so Agnes and Betike could not hear mass or receive communion. But together with three Franciscan nuns, they carried on a semblance of convent life, spending their days praying and meditating. On Christmas Eve, they celebrated by setting up a crèche, a model of the stable where Jesus Christ was said to have been born. Finally, in early January, they sailed into the Bay of Bengal and landed in Calcutta.

Calcutta, India's third largest city, must have been a staggering sight for a young woman accustomed to the quiet countryside and open fields of eastern Europe. Carts, animals, and ragged-looking

Beside a sleeping beggar a calf roams the filthy streets of a Calcutta slum. After a six-week stay in Ireland, where she studied English, Agnes Bojaxhiu arrived in Calcutta in January 1929.

people thronged the streets. To Agnes, Dublin had been a busy metropolis, but Calcutta was all chaos and clamor. The enormous, largely uneducated population of Calcutta earned most of its paltry income (perhaps a few cents a day) by desperately trying to sell goods or services to the few residents who could afford them. Men worked as human horses, pulling *rickshas* — small, covered two-wheeled carriages — through the narrow streets. The overcrowded city contained slums with horrible living conditions that challenged even the strongest individuals. In these slums, the average life span at the time of Agnes Bojaxhiu's arrival in India was only 30 years.

Agnes, however, caught only a brief glimpse of Calcutta before she was sent to the Loreto sisters in northern India. The order kept a convent in Darjeeling, in the foothills of the Himalayas. In May 1929, in the stunning beauty and peace of the magnificent mountains, Agnes's novitiate began. She studied Scripture and the rules of the Loreto order. She took more English lessons and began to study the Indian languages of Hindi and Bengali. She received instruction in teaching, for that was the duty of the Loreto sisters. Along with the nuns, she practiced the arts of meditation and silence. She also taught at the convent school, where she instructed European and Indian children for two hours a day. Agnes did all that was asked of her with a simple, sincere heart.

On May 24, 1931, Agnes Bojaxhiu took her first vows as a nun. As a Loreto sister, she vowed herself to poverty, chastity, and obedience, prostrating herself with her whole body and face to the floor. In a ceremony much like a wedding, complete with white dress and veil, she symbolically married Christ and became Sister Teresa. She had chosen the name after Thérèse, the patron saint of missionaries. Known as the Little Flower of Jesus, the 19th-century nun from Lisieux, France, had spent her life in an obscure convent before she died of tuberculosis at the age of 24. She believed that she could best serve God by leading a life of goodness and simplicity and held that even the most menial or

Agnes sent her relatives this picture, taken in 1930, of herself as a novice in Darjeeling. The following year, Agnes took her first vows. Adopting the name of a 19th-century French nun, she became Sister Teresa.

Children play in front of the hovels that are their homes in Calcutta. Sister Teresa's first assignment was teaching at the Calcutta convent school called Loreto Entally. The convent walls largely insulated her from the poverty of the sprawling city.

outwardly demeaning tasks were forms of worship provided they were done to help others or to serve God. Like Saint Thérèse of Lisieux, Sister Teresa longed to express her faith by going "the way of spiritual childhood, the way of trust and absolute self-surrender" to the will of God.

Sister Teresa's first assignment was at the Loreto convent in Entally, a district of Calcutta. The Loreto order had been teaching Indian and Anglo-Indian girls since the mid-19th century and was well known in Calcutta. The spacious convent school buildings were isolated from the poverty of the surrounding city by gardens and stone walls. At the convent school, popularly called Loreto Entally, Sister Teresa taught geography and history to students from relatively wealthy families. On the same grounds was located St. Mary's, a school for younger children from all different classes, including some orphans whom the sisters cared for. Sister Teresa's duties at St. Mary's provided an opportunity for her to hone her knowledge of the Bengali language.

On May 14, 1937, Teresa took her final vows, pledging to serve God for the rest of her life. She eventually became principal of her school, but her attention kept straying beyond the walls of the convent. She loved her girls, and she loved teaching, but the question remained, "Is this where God really wants me?" Sister Teresa's bedroom window faced the teeming area of slums known as Motijhil. The stark contrast between the school's stately buildings and the squalor beyond the convent gates touched the young nun.

Standing in the darkness of her room, overlooking the slum, Sister Teresa often witnessed the suffering of its inhabitants. Disease, starvation, and misery abounded on the other side of the convent wall. She wanted to go and help, but the order's rule of enclosure meant that no nun left the convent unless she was desperately ill and needed hospital care or was bound for the annual retreat at Darjeeling.

During the years of Teresa's enclosure at Loreto, India was undergoing momentous changes. Mohandas Gandhi was leading a movement aimed at

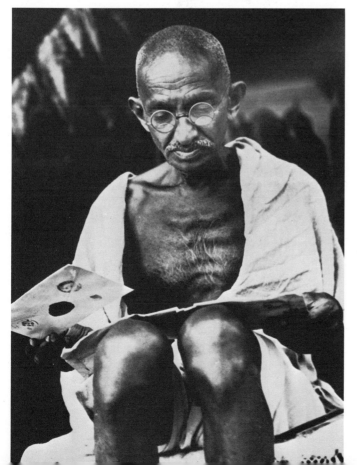

Mohandas Gandhi, known as *Mahatma* — the Hindu word for Great Soul — was the leader of the Indian independence movement of the 1930s and 1940s. Promoting nonviolent resistance, he mobilized millions of Indians against British colonial rule.

freeing India from British colonial rule. Gandhi and his millions of followers used nonviolent forms of protest in their battle for self-government.

As the struggle for Indian independence heated up, tensions between the two largest religious groups, Hindus and Muslims, began to erupt into violence. The minority Muslims, fearing that they would become the victims of discrimination in a state ruled by Hindus, began to demand an independent state for themselves. The Hindus rejected this idea of partitioning India. In August 1946, a massive four-day riot between the warring factions erupted in Calcutta. Daily life, including food deliveries to the Loreto compound, ground to a halt as the streets turned into battlefields. As principal, Sister Teresa was responsible for feeding the several hundred girls at Loreto Entally, and despite the danger, she felt it her duty to go out and find them something to eat. The stark reality of the streets, from which she was so sheltered in the convent, assaulted her senses as she made her way through

Bodies litter the streets of Calcutta in the aftermath of the August 1946 Hindu-Muslim riots, in which 5,000 people died. Because the rioting cut off supplies to the Loreto school, Sister Teresa braved the streets to find food for her students.

the city. The riots took the lives of 5,000 Calcuttans, and approximately 15,000 more were injured. The bodies of hundreds of victims of the Hindu-Muslim conflict lay unclaimed in the streets. Sister Teresa was appalled and frightened by the carnage around her, but she continued her quest. Finally, some soldiers gave her several bags of rice and led her back to the convent, warning her to stay off the streets.

Perhaps this gruesome glimpse of the streets of Calcutta intensified Sister Teresa's desire to work in the slums. On September 10, 1946, aboard a train traveling to the Loreto convent in Darjeeling for her annual retreat, she experienced what she later termed "the call within a call." She was now convinced that God wanted her to give up her comfortable convent life and go into the slums to reach the poor. Sister Teresa felt that God's message was unmistakable: "I was to leave the convent and help the poor while living among them. It was an order. To fail it would have been to break the faith." But to avoid breaking her own faith, she would have to break a promise she had made 15 years ago, when she pledged her life to the Loreto order. She consulted with Father Celeste Van Exem, the Belgian Jesuit priest who was her spiritual director. He advised her to let him bring her request to Calcutta's archbishop Ferdinand Perier at an opportune moment.

Near the end of 1946, Father Van Exem approached the archbishop. Perier was hesitant to allow Sister Teresa to leave her order, especially to go out into the slums to work with the poor and start a new congregation. He told Father Van Exem, "You don't know your Sister Teresa as I know her. I knew her when she was a novice in Darjeeling. When she was a novice, she couldn't even light the candles . . . and you want to make her the superior of a congregation! She's not able to do that." He concluded that the matter should be set aside for a year.

Sister Teresa obediently accepted the archbishop's decision. She was sent about 300 miles to Asansol to be in charge of the gardens and kitchen at the Loreto convent there. While she was there, Arch-

Novices read prayers from a Bible. Sister Teresa loved the calm religious life of the Loreto convent. Leaving it to work among Calcutta's poor, she later said, was harder than leaving her home and family as a young girl.

bishop Perier conferred with other priests. He wanted their opinions on the practicality of Sister Teresa's plan.

When the year drew to a close, Archbishop Perier gave Sister Teresa permission to write to the mother general of the Loreto order. When she showed him the letter, the archbishop insisted that she change one vital word. She had asked for *exclaustration*, which meant she would still be a nun under vows of obedience, poverty, and chastity, but free to travel wherever she felt she was needed. He insisted that she substitute the word *secularization*, which meant that she would no longer be a nun. Sister Teresa was dismayed: If she was no longer a member of the clergy, she could not set up an order and have other nuns help her in her charity work. However, Sister Teresa firmly believed in the authority of the church, and she once again obediently followed the guidance of her superiors, changing her request to secularization. She was determined to go to the poor at any cost. When the mother general wrote back giving her permission to appeal to the church's highest officials in Rome, she told Sister Teresa to ask for exclaustration, not secularization. Again, Archbishop Perier refused to send the letter to Rome unless she asked for secularization. By rewriting the letter as he asked, Sister Teresa proved her utmost obedience.

Archbishop Perier sent her letter along with one of his own in February 1947. Six months later, word from Rome finally arrived. An amazing fact became clear as Father Van Exem and Archbishop Perier read the decree. Sister Teresa had been granted the exclaustration she had prayed for.

Father Celeste Van Exem, a Belgian Jesuit priest, was spiritual adviser to the Loreto nuns in Calcutta. From the time Sister Teresa first decided to leave her order to work in the slums, Van Exem provided much-needed emotional, as well as practical, support.

3

Answering the Call

On August 16, 1948, Sister Teresa removed the dark Loreto habit she had worn every day for 17 years. In the stifling, filthy streets of the slums there would be no place for the traditional long robes, stiff collars, and elaborate head coverings usually worn by the nuns. Instead, Sister Teresa put on a simple white cotton *sari* — the traditional garment worn by most women in India — that was decorated with a blue border. The sari would eventually become the habit of her new congregation. She was ready to leave the confines of Loreto's convents and venture out into the world she was to serve.

Although she had been working toward this day for nearly two years, her departure was very painful. She later called leaving the Loreto convent "my greatest sacrifice, the most difficult thing I have ever done." She had lived and served with the Loreto nuns longer than she had dwelled in her native village of Skopje. The sisters were her friends and companions, the only ones she knew. Only the firmest belief in God's plan for her life could cause her to uproot herself once again.

Before Sister Teresa left, she told her plans to the superior of Entally, Sister Cenacle. The nun had worked with and depended upon Sister Teresa for many years and often referred to Sister Teresa as

The loneliness of those first days . . . is unimaginable. For someone long accustomed to life lived with a beloved community, where every day had its preordained pattern, the uncharted day must have been dizzying. In addition, the conviction of being strange and unique must have been painful in the extreme.
—EILEEN EGAN
American author and Co-Worker, on Mother Teresa's departure from Loreto

Malnourished children cling to their mother's skirt in the city of Patna, India. Before she embarked on her mission to the "poorest of the poor," Sister Teresa traveled to Patna to receive basic medical training from Mother Dengel and her Medical Missionary Sisters.

her "right arm." As Drana Bojaxhiu had done 20 years before, Sister Cenacle cried over Sister Teresa's departure but consoled herself with the belief that Sister Teresa was following God's will.

When she first left the Loreto convent, Sister Teresa was not bound directly for the teeming streets of Calcutta. Instead, she headed for Patna, 240 miles away, in order to receive medical training from Mother Anna Dengel and her Medical Missionary Sisters. Mother Dengel herself had fought to obtain church approval for her nuns to establish an order to serve the people directly. The Medical Missionary Sisters went to local homes and hospitals, where they did everything from delivering babies to performing surgery.

As the train to Patna crossed the Hooghly River over the huge bridge that connects Calcutta and its twin city, Howrah, Sister Teresa caught a glimpse of the thousands of destitute, starving people who would fill her future. When the train finally arrived

Wearing the blue-bordered *sari* that has become the habit of her order, Mother Teresa attends to patients. Even when she first worked among the sick during her training with the Medical Missionary Sisters, she displayed the compassion that would be her trademark in later years.

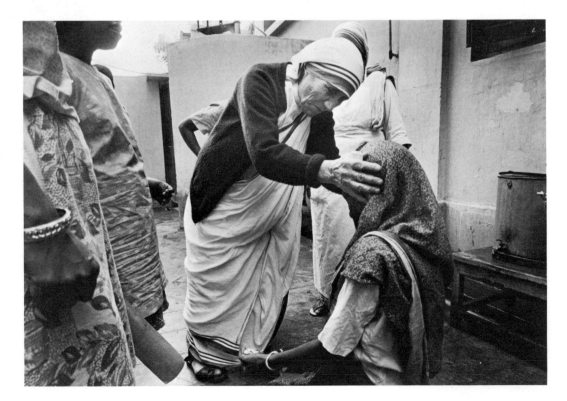

in Patna, the sisters warmly welcomed Sister Teresa and helped her settle in. Almost immediately, they began calling her in to assist them. Sister Teresa learned by doing. The nuns handled dozens of cases every day, so there was no time for detailed instruction.

Sister Teresa lived and worked in Patna for three months. There she learned how to deliver babies, set broken bones, and administer inoculations. She became acquainted with various illnesses and their effects and studied the fundamentals of nutrition and hygiene.

As Sister Teresa worked alongside the sisters at Patna, they got to know her well. When she told them that she planned to subsist each day on rice and salt, the common diet of Calcutta's poorest citizens, they advised her against it. Mother Dengel warned her that such a diet would only sap her strength and endanger her life. Sister Teresa saw the wisdom of the advice and gave up her idealistic plan; she and the young women she hoped would join her were to eat a balanced diet to keep up their strength.

The Medical Missionary Sisters were surprised at how quickly Sister Teresa adapted to her work. Instead of being overwhelmed by the staggering work load and depressed by the daily exposure to illness and misery, she buckled down and decided that her priority was to be wherever she was needed most. She seemed to have the ability to shut out worries of red tape, reprisals, and expenses in order to concentrate on the immediate task.

Having gleaned enough knowledge to begin work in the streets of Calcutta, Sister Teresa left Patna one morning in December 1948. She traveled alone back over the Howrah Bridge and down into the city, where she knew without a doubt that God wanted her to spend her life. She arrived with no money and nowhere to stay. She got in touch with Father Van Exem, who contacted St. Joseph's Home, where a group of nuns called the Little Sisters of the Poor took in destitute elderly people. He asked if Sister Teresa could live there while she conducted her mis-

This steel bridge spans the Hooghly River to link Calcutta with its twin city, Howrah. Sister Teresa viewed the overpopulated slums of Calcutta as her train passed over the bridge in August 1948 on its way to Patna.

sions of mercy within Calcutta. The order's mother superior gladly received her.

Sister Teresa took a short time to settle in and to seek Father Van Exem's advice on how to begin her work. Where to start in a city the size of Calcutta, with the overwhelming needs of its immense population, was a daunting problem. She spent her first few days in Calcutta praying, studying, and helping the Little Sisters of the Poor as they worked with their charges.

Finally, on December 21, 1948, Sister Teresa ventured out into the streets to begin her mission. She packed a lunch and headed into the slums without money, companions, or even a plan of action. The 38-year-old nun had renounced all material comforts, even the security of a daily schedule.

She walked for about an hour until she reached Motijhil, the slum she had long observed from her bedroom window in the Loreto convent. Her training was as a teacher, so she decided that her first act would be to start a school in Motijhil. On the first day, five children went to her "school," an open space under a tiny tree near the hovels of the poor. Her "classroom," to which the half-naked and unkempt children came, had no desks, blackboards, or books. Working outside and scratching lessons in the dirt with a stick, Sister Teresa began with the basics and taught the children the alphabet. The next day, attendance doubled, and in very little time, almost 40 pupils gathered around her each day. As they recited their lessons, their young voices could be heard echoing through the overcrowded streets.

Although they were eager to learn, the children had no background on which to build concepts of letters and numbers. The challenge Sister Teresa took on as a teacher in the slums far surpassed that of instructing the girls who had attended the Loreto convent school. Sister Teresa's determination to help the poor pushed her to labor long hours. Under her able direction, her students learned not only language and number basics, but sanitation and hygiene, as well.

Oh God, you are all! Use me as you will. You made me leave the convent where I was at least of some use. Now guide me as you wish.

—MOTHER TERESA
for guidance upon starting
her work among
Calcutta's poor

42

Sister Teresa knew that the good her school did was just a drop in the bucket. Calcutta's dire economic situation had worsened over the past few years. In 1947, India had finally gained independence from Great Britain, but the insoluble differences between the two main religious groups had led to the partitioning (division) of the country into the Muslim state of Pakistan, which occupied the northwest and northeast corners, and the predominantly Hindu nation of India. As a result of the horrible fighting between the religious factions and the partitioning of the country, millions were uprooted from their homes and stripped of their incomes and property. Fearing the growing violence, nearly 7 million Muslims left India, while about 5.5 million Hindus fled the new nation of Pakistan. This mass migration was accompanied by horrible riots and bloodshed on both sides. The Hindus streamed south, and many of them settled in Calcutta, where they swelled the already overcrowded *bustees*, or slums. They came with nothing, seeking any way to earn money. Doomed to a lifetime of extreme poverty, they lived on the streets, sleeping, cooking, eating, and often dying there.

Students learn their lessons at an outdoor school in Lahore, India, in 1925. Strapped for funds but determined to educate Calcutta's poor children, Sister Teresa began her own outdoor school, scratching lessons in the dirt with a stick in a Calcutta slum called Motijhil.

Refugees driven from their homes by religiously motivated violence stand guard over their possessions as they await transport to new homes. The partitioning of India in 1947 caused mass rioting and migration as Muslims fled north to the new nation of Pakistan, and Hindus streamed south into India.

Food and drinking water became scarce, and the already overtaxed sanitation system could not keep up with the sudden increase in population. The only things that seemed to thrive in Calcutta's slums were disease-carrying insects and bacteria. Unsanitary conditions prevailed everywhere. Water from the polluted river was pumped into the public water supply. Because of a lack of toilet facilities, people were forced to urinate on the street. Insects abounded, laying eggs on food sources as well as anything else inhabitable.

Through her dealings with her students, Sister Teresa came into contact with their families, many of whom had lost their source of income because the father had succumbed to illness. Medical care in Calcutta was woefully inadequate. In *City of Joy*, Dominique Lapierre tells of one man who injured his foot while pulling his ricksha. The injury, though painful, was not severe. Yet when he finally received care at a horribly overcrowded local hospital, his foot was amputated. Infection set in, and the man died. In Calcutta, thousands of residents perished each year because they did not receive adequate medical attention.

The depth of poverty that the city's destitute faced every day appalled Sister Teresa. They considered it good fortune to obtain even 1 *rupee* a day (about 11 U.S. cents) for their daily needs. Often they were not able to earn any money at all, and after a day spent scrounging for work, they would go to bed on the street or in a tiny, dirty hovel. With each new dawn, they faced gnawing hunger and growing hopelessness.

Sister Teresa did not have any money to give; instead she gave daily of herself, of her time and energy, her love and compassion. She walked the streets looking for ways to help, returning each evening depleted and fatigued, having no idea how she would get through the next day. The task seemed impossible. Nearly everyone she saw needed immediate assistance. Rather than succumb to feelings of despair, though, Sister Teresa dipped into the reserves of her faith in God. Years later, she

A barefoot teenager pulls a *ricksha* through the streets of Calcutta. Although many of the city's poor work long days to earn money, most find it nearly impossible to earn a decent wage.

explained how she faced the overwhelming poverty of the slums. She declared that she saw Jesus Christ "in the broken bodies of forgotten people." With each individual she helped, she believed she was repaying a debt to God. Eileen Egan, author of a biography of Mother Teresa entitled *Such a Vision of the Street*, recorded an incident from one of Sister Teresa's first trips out: "I picked up a man from the street, and he was eaten up alive from worms," Mother Teresa reported. "Nobody could stand him, and he was smelling so badly. I went to him to clean him and he asked, 'Why do you do this?' I said, 'Because I love you.' "

At the end of each long day, after walking an hour back to St. Joseph's, Sister Teresa welcomed a warm meal and sleep. Sometimes before falling asleep, she would remember the comfortable routine at Loreto, the celebration of mass with the other sisters, and the time spent in meditation. In her diary of those first days she wrote, "God wants me to be a lonely nun, laden with the poverty of the cross. Today I learned a good lesson. The poverty of the poor is so hard. When I was going and going until my legs and arms were paining, I was thinking how they have to suffer to get food and shelter. Then the comfort of Loreto came to tempt me. But God, out of love for you, and by my own free choice, I desire to do whatever be your holy will. Give me courage now, this moment."

As the days went on, the two hours spent walking to and from St. Joseph's each day seemed a waste of precious time. With Father Van Exem's help, she found a place to stay closer to her work. In February 1949 a small room on the second floor of 14 Creek Lane became her new home. The house belonged to Michael Gomes, an Indian-Catholic teacher. The Gomes family became extremely helpful to Sister Teresa; Michael would obtain medicine for her, and Mabel, his daughter, often accompanied her on shopping trips to buy supplies. Their moral support was indispensable, for it made Sister Teresa feel less alone.

Sister Teresa's new headquarters were spartan.

She furnished her room with wooden boxes for chairs and a packing crate for a desk. She hung a picture of the Virgin Mary on the wall. No one realized it at the time, of course, but this tiny, obscure room was destined to become the cradle of an influential worldwide organization.

In March 1949 one of Sister Teresa's students from Entally arrived at 14 Creek Lane. She had come seeking her former teacher and principal from the Loreto school. Subhasini Das could not forget Sister Teresa; she wanted to join her mentor in her work with the poor in Calcutta. In this act of love, she became the first of hundreds of young women who gave up security and material possessions to help India's poorest of the poor.

Mother Teresa comforts an ailing man. Her solitary efforts in Calcutta were given a boost when some of her former students joined her in 1949. Sister Teresa welcomed the help of Calcutta church officials to obtain Vatican recognition of the Missionaries of Charity as an official order.

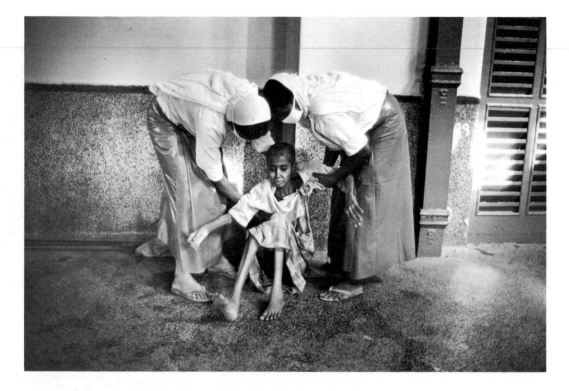

Limbs weakened by disease and malnutrition, a child attempts to stand with the assistance of two nuns. Mother Teresa was deeply gratified by the faith and dedication of the growing numbers of young women who joined in her work.

Not long afterward, a graduate of St. Mary's, Magdalena Gomes, also came to Sister Teresa. Much to the dismay of her parents, she had left the convent school before completing her senior year and final exams. Sister Teresa, along with all her other work, made sure Magdalena completed her courses and helped her pass final exams. She always made certain that the young women who came to her finished their education.

Never knowing what type of situation they might encounter, the three women would go into the streets together after praying for courage and endurance. They went from house to house begging for contributions, then used the money to feed and treat the hungry and sick and to support their school. Every day they were confronted with filthy, diseased, and starving people who desperately needed help. Caught up in her work, Sister Teresa hardly noticed that her first year of exclaustration had ended.

Archbishop Perier now had to decide if Sister Teresa could remain outside the convent. Evidently, good reports on her work had reached the archbishop, for he would not consider making Sister Teresa give up her mission to rejoin the convent life. If she had to return, the young women who had joined her, now 10 in number, would also have to enter the convent. Perier also noted that Sister Teresa had chosen to become an Indian citizen in 1949, demonstrating in yet another way her dedication to her mission. In her book *A Gift for God*, Mother Teresa later wrote, "I feel Indian to the most profound depths of my soul."

Archbishop Perier decided to help Sister Teresa and the dedicated young women who followed her in their quest to obtain official designation as a congregation under his archdiocese. This plan would give Sister Teresa an independent status that would aid her work tremendously. He told Father Van Exem that if an acceptable constitution could be written quickly, he would take it with him on his upcoming trip to Rome and present it to the church's Office for the Propagation of the Faith.

Sister Teresa drew up a satisfactory constitution that included the original three vows of poverty, chastity, and obedience as well as a fourth vow of "wholehearted free service to the poorest of the poor." Not one to dwell on the legalities and intricacies of the constitution, Sister Teresa stressed, "In the choice of works, there was neither planning nor preconceived ideas. We started our work as the suffering of the people called us. God showed us what to do."

Cardinal Pietro Fumosoni-Biondi, head of the Office for the Propagation of the Faith, accepted the constitution. On October 7, 1950, Sister Teresa became the mother superior of a new order called the Missionaries of Charity. Although her official title was now Reverend Mother, she refused the adjective *reverend*, desiring to be called simply Mother Teresa. The ceremony took place in a third floor room of 14 Creek Lane. Several of the Medical Missionary Sisters from Patna attended, and Archbishop Perier

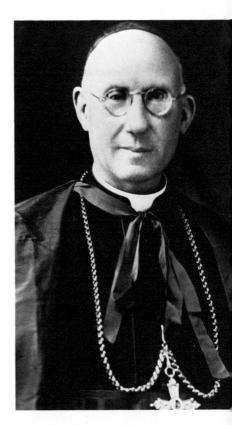

In 1950 Italian cardinal Pietro Fumosoni-Biondi, the head of the Roman Catholic Office for the Propagation of the Faith, approved Sister Teresa's plans for her own order. She became the mother superior of the Missionaries of Charity.

and Father Van Exem officiated. A decree written by Mother Teresa outlining the duties of the new order was read aloud:

> To fulfill our mission of compassion and love to the poorest of the poor we go:
> — seeking out in towns and villages all over the world even amid squalid surroundings the poorest, the abandoned, the sick, the infirm, the leprosy patients, the dying, the desperate, the lost, the outcasts;
> — taking care of them,
> — rendering help to them,
> — visiting them assiduously,
> — living Christ's love for them, and
> — awakening their response to his great love.

When Subhasini Das, Mother Teresa's first follower, took her vows, she adopted the name of Agnes, Mother Teresa's first name. When she first

Wearing a surgical mask to protect herself from germs, a nun checks on patients in a Missionaries of Charity hospice in Calcutta. Mother Teresa knew that joining her order meant a very difficult life, and she made sure the young women who came to her were prepared to give up everything for the poor.

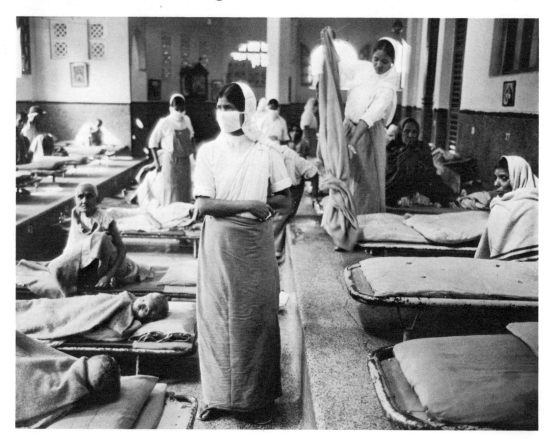

came to work with Mother Teresa, she had told her former teacher about others from St. Mary's who also wanted to join her. These girls had heard much about Mother Teresa's work, and they wanted to share the burdens with her.

The girls from St. Mary's came to Teresa steadily, sometimes dropping out of their classes at Loreto before their final exams, as Magdalena Gomes had done. Like Magdalena, who became Sister Gertrude, they had to complete their studies and final exams under Mother Teresa's guidance. The dedicated band of women grew to 26, and the Gomes family kindly allowed the use of more of their large house.

As her new congregation of nuns grew, Mother Teresa continued to teach each one how to care for the sick and dying. She encouraged them to treat each person as God's child. In *A Gift for God*, she tells her novices: "Speak tenderly to them. Let there be kindness in your face, in your eyes, in your smile, in the warmth of your greeting. Always have a cheerful smile. Don't only give your care, but give your heart as well."

Mother Teresa insisted that the nuns who joined her maintain cheerful dispositions as they worked to alleviate misery. "The poor," she said, "deserve not only service and dedication but also the joy that belongs to human love," as an antidote to the unrelenting misery they endured day after day. In a pamphlet describing the many qualifications young women needed to join her order, Mother Teresa wrote that would-be missionaries must be "possessed of a good sense of humor." Although this is difficult when one considers the agony the Missionaries of Charity often witnessed, many applicants joined her. Mother Teresa welcomed them, although she always warned them, "It will be a hard life."

> *Even in the beginning, I never asked for money. I wanted to serve the poor simply for love of God. I wanted the poor to receive free what the rich get for themselves with money.*
> —MOTHER TERESA

4

Within the City

Four years after Mother Teresa answered the call she heard on the train to Darjeeling, the Missionaries of Charity had become a reality. The girls who were coming to Mother Teresa did not care that they would have a hard life. They came because they were willing to share a life filled with poverty and sacrifice for the sake of helping others. Like Mother Teresa, their vocation, or religious calling, was to assist the most needy. As Mother Teresa explained it, "Vocation is like a little seed. It has to be nourished. You have to keep on looking out for it. Vocation cannot be forced. The person whom Christ has chosen for Himself, she knows — maybe she doesn't know how to express it, but she knows."

When they arrived in Calcutta to join the Missionaries of Charity, some of the novices expected that the hardships of the slums would carry over into their living accommodations and diets. But Mother Teresa had learned her lesson from the sisters at Patna: At each meal, she made sure that her nuns had plenty to eat. Their rooms were simple but reasonably comfortable.

Even though several sisters shared each room they were allotted on the upper floor of the Gomes house, the Missionaries of Charity soon required more space. Father Julien Henry, a Belgian Jesuit

> *Mother trained her young sisters by word and example, as Jesus had done with his apostles at the Last Supper. She told them how they were to treat the poorest of the poor, in whom they were to see Jesus, their Lord and master.*
> —EDWARD LE JOLY
> Belgian Jesuit priest and spiritual adviser to the Missionaries of Charity

A homeless man sleeps in a Calcutta doorway. The Missionaries of Charity seek not only to help the sick and hungry, but to restore human dignity. "The poor," Mother Teresa has said, "deserve not only service and dedication, but also the joy that belongs to human love."

priest who was the head of a parish church in Calcutta and had become Mother Teresa's trusted adviser and ally, rode his bicycle around the city, looking for a bigger building to house the missionaries.

Father Henry remembered a Muslim politician he had met who owned a large Calcutta home in which he had planned to live after retirement. He had changed his mind, however, because of the upheavals between the religious factions and decided to sell it and leave Calcutta. His home on 54A Lower Circular Road suited the needs of the Missionaries of Charity well, and Archbishop Perier lent them the money to buy the 3-story structure. As Mother Teresa later commented, "Divine providence is always given us in unexpected ways."

By mid-1953 the Missionaries of Charity had moved into their new home on Lower Circular Road and designated the residence as the new official headquarters of the organization. During this time, Mother Teresa took her final vows as mother superior of her new order, and four novices professed their first vows as Missionaries of Charity. Mother Teresa still refused to be called Reverend Mother; in fact, she never set herself above her sisters. Their work was her work, whether it was scrubbing a floor on hands and knees, washing mounds of bedding by hand, or cleaning maggots out of a putrid wound. Mother Teresa has described some of their charges as "filthy, covered with sores, eaten up with syphilis. We wash them all. Of course, when a case is really too bad, I do it myself."

One day in 1954, Mother Teresa found a woman dying in the gutter. When she brought the woman to a nearby hospital, the medical officials were reluctant to take in another obviously destitute and hopeless patient. Mother Teresa was adamant: "I told them that I would stay at the hospital until they took her, and so to get rid of me I think they took the woman." That same day, Mother Teresa approached Calcutta's public health authorities and asked their assistance in providing the city's poor with a decent place to die.

> *By her care, she was asserting that a spark [of life] was of infinite value, issuing from an infinite Creator. The person, no matter how disfigured, mattered.*
>
> —EILEEN EGAN
> author and Co-Worker, on
> Mother Teresa's work at
> the Home for the Dying

Soon after, a city official contacted the Missionaries of Charity with good news: He knew of an unused building that could serve as a shelter for dying destitutes. The building adjoined an important Hindu shrine to the goddess Kali and had been used to provide overnight accommodations for pilgrims who had come long distances to worship at the temple. Built like an inn around a courtyard, the structure seemed perfect for the sisters' purpose.

Twenty-four hours later, the Missionaries of Charity began to transform the building into *Nirmal Hriday*, Place of the Immaculate Heart. Some Hindu leaders objected to the idea of Catholic nuns setting up a home on the site of a Hindu shrine. The sisters, however, did not attempt to convert their patients; they were concerned only that the poor brought to them were allowed to die with dignity. Hindus, Muslims, and Christians all received the rituals prescribed for the dying by their respective faiths. After visiting the compound, a skeptical Hindu leader was filled with admiration for the project — and the nun who oversaw it. He told his followers, "In the temple you have a goddess in stone; [in Mother Teresa] you have a living goddess."

Patients look on as nuns scrub the floors at *Nirmal Hriday*, the Home for the Dying, founded by Mother Teresa in 1954. Moved by the sight of dead and dying people in Calcutta's streets, Mother Teresa opened the shelter to help the poor die with dignity.

The intricately carved roof of this Hindu temple towers over a city street. As they ministered to the poor, the Missionaries of Charity occasionally encountered the distrust and resentment of the nation's non-Christian majority, who feared that the missionaries would try to convert Indians to Catholicism.

Each morning Mother Teresa and her sisters walked through the city streets looking for those who most needed their assistance. Calcutta's police force also brought many desperately ill paupers to Nirmal Hriday. The building could accommodate approximately 120 men and women at a time. Over the years, tens of thousands of people have been admitted to Nirmal Hriday, and about half of them have died there. The Missionaries of Charity have sought to provide these individuals with "beautiful deaths." Mother Teresa explained, "A beautiful death is for people who lived like animals, to die like angels—loved and wanted."

Inside the home, also referred to as *Kalighat* — the Home for the Dying — rows and rows of low, narrow beds hold men and women whose faces mirror suffering and pain. Tuberculosis, malaria, dysentery, malnutrition, leprosy, and cancer are just a few of the causes of death within its walls. In every account of life and death inside Kalighat, Mother Teresa's love and respect for the ill and dying are evident. As he neared the end, one man who had spent much of his life on the streets proclaimed, "Now, I can die like a human being." The sisters work hour after hour, every day, holding hands, washing diseased bodies, and offering any kind of comfort they can.

As they ministered to the poor in Calcutta, the nuns repeatedly encountered starving and homeless children. It was not unusual to find newborn babies, especially females, in refuse dumps. Many Indians considered baby girls less valuable than male offspring because they needed to be provided with a dowry (payment) to marry. They then left their home, thus depriving the family of desperately needed labor. Many of the abandoned children were premature or diseased, blind, or handicapped in some other way. Other children were casualties of broken families, separated from the ones they loved and put out on the street to beg. Often, when a poor woman died at Nirmal Hriday, she left behind children. The sisters cared for such orphans.

Mother Teresa works among patients at a Missionaries of Charity ward. Although she has hundreds of helpers, she continues to administer personally to the sick. "It is Christ you tend in the poor," she has said. "It is his wounds you bathe, his sores you clean, his limbs you bandage."

Because of the large numbers of children the Missionaries of Charity found, Mother Teresa felt compelled to open a home for them, as well. In 1955 a rough two-story building, quite close to the order's headquarters, opened up for rental. As soon as Mother Teresa could rent and furnish the building, *Nirmala Shishu Bhavan*, the Children's Home of the Immaculate Heart, became a haven for children who had no home.

Space within the new home was partitioned in order to provide the best use. Cribs holding infants

A young Calcutta girl holds an infant. In 1955, the Missionaries of Charity opened *Nirmala Shishu Bhavan*, the Children's Home of the Immaculate Heart, to care for abandoned children.

who had survived several months at Shishu Bhavan lined the walls on the lower floor. These babies, as well as the older children who sat on the floor, were relatively healthy. They were tended by novices preparing for their vows. Their clothing and toys were donated by the community. In another room tiny babies, sometimes three to a crib, fought with death. The pumping sound of life-support systems alerted every visitor to the seriousness of the children's situations. In this room, around-the-clock care helped some infants survive.

In addition to housing ill and destitute children, Mother Teresa and the sisters at Shishu Bhavan set up a food-distribution program for the hungry. Families were given different-colored pieces of paper, depending on their religion, so that the Muslims all came on a certain day, the Hindus on

Mother Teresa plays with orphaned boys and girls at Nirmala Shishu Bhavan. She and the sisters not only attend to physical needs but also seek to rekindle the curiosity and joy that many of these children have lost while living in the slum streets.

another day. Given the desperation with which the thousands of starving people sought the food, Mother Teresa displayed great foresight in keeping the often antagonistic religious groups separate.

Shishu Bhavan also became home for the teen-aged girls who, having lost the protection of their families through death or desertion, otherwise would have become victims of rape or been driven to a life of prostitution. These older girls often helped out with the younger children at Shishu Bhavan and were taught useful skills, such as sewing and typing, so they would be able to take care of themselves. Whenever one of the girls received an acceptable marriage proposal, Mother Teresa saw to it that she had at least some small dowry, even if only a simple bed and some towels, to take with her.

The work at Shishu Bhavan was exhausting and sometimes fruitless. Some critics contended that the funds spent nursing pauper children would have been better spent on drastic population control programs. But Mother Teresa disagreed: "God gives what is needed. He gives to the flowers, to the birds, and little children his life. There are never enough of them. God made the world rich enough to feed and clothe all human beings."

Mother Teresa's heart was also touched by the plight of another segment of Calcutta's society — the victims of leprosy. Hansen's disease, as leprosy is officially termed, has ravaged humankind for centuries; the despised, neglected leper is a familiar figure in the Bible. The bacterial disease destroys skin and nerve tissues and if not detected and treated, results in severe deformities, especially of the extremities. Hands and feet become stumps; noses waste away. Dangerous infections occur in the diseased skin, and gangrene, the death of tissue, can spread rapidly, requiring amputation to stop it. Although the disease is not highly contagious, lepers were often treated as outcasts, even by their own families. To the Hindus in India, lepers were thought to have done some very evil deed in a past life to bring such a miserable existence upon themselves.

In 1957 approximately 30,000 lepers lived in Calcutta. Chased away from their homes and jobs, five leprosy sufferers sought out the one person they knew would care: Mother Teresa. She had already thought of the need to minister to the lepers, but the visit by the tiny, pitiful group seemed to be an indication to her to begin an active program to aid all lepers.

Mother Teresa knew that sulfone drugs and a proper diet could result in improvement within a year of prompt treatment in nearly all leprosy patients. Indeed, the disease was curable if caught in time. Many leprosy sufferers, especially those who had lost feet to the disease, found it almost impossible to walk any distance to a leper asylum. Many leprous women, embarrassed to be seen by a male

A man in Delhi, India, shows the results of untreated Hansen's disease, popularly known as leprosy. Mother Teresa found that fear of contamination and revulsion at the disease's disfiguring effects left many lepers outcasts. Helping them became a special concern of the Missionaries of Charity.

doctor, avoided treatment. So Mother Teresa determined to bring the treatment to the lepers.

The Missionaries of Charity set up several clinics at key places in the city and equipped a van with medicines, food, disinfectants, bandages, and other necessary supplies. With two sisters and a doctor, Mother Teresa rode into the narrow streets to find infected families. Once they had been found and treated, the lepers were given identification cards. The doctor started a file on each patient, and provisions, usually powdered milk, rice, and medication, were handed out. Every week at the same time and place, the lepers lined up and patiently waited to be seen.

Because the government had shut down the original hospital for lepers in Calcutta, the Missionaries of Charity opened rehabilitation centers for them. One of these centers, built of corrugated tin, sat

Mother Teresa talks to a victim of Hansen's disease as a volunteer plays soothing music. After the Missionaries of Charity set up stationary centers for the treatment of leprosy, they established mobile clinics to bring aid to those lepers who could not walk or would not come out in public.

precariously close to a railroad track in an industrial area of the city. Evidently the passing trains that continually shook the buildings did not bother the Missionaries of Charity. The location was not as important to them as the love and care they gave.

Another outgrowth of Mother Teresa's efforts for the lepers was *Shanti Nagar*, the Town of Peace. A community of rehabilitating lepers, it covers 35 acres about 200 miles outside Calcutta. The approximately 400 families who live there today are largely self-supporting, thanks to Mother Teresa's foresight in training the lepers in skills such as brick making and handicrafts. Shanti Nagar is run independently of the Missionaries of Charity, but it continues to achieve the goals of its founder. Every day, the people there are not just sustained but enriched by a program that acknowledges their importance as individuals. This attitude has always remained at the core of Mother Teresa's work: Each individual has equal worth in the eyes of God and deserves recognition as a valuable human being.

A Missionaries of Charity nun walks through the narrow courtyards of Calcutta's backstreets, which are crowded with livestock as well as people. Mother Teresa and her helpers fight a daily battle against the unsanitary conditions that result from the city's severe overcrowding.

5

The Mission Expands

Mother Teresa once said, "Calcutta can be found all over the world if you have eyes to see." Across the globe, there are unwanted, neglected people. Rejected by society or forgotten by family and friends, they suffer the greatest poverty — loneliness. Unable to ignore such suffering once she became aware of it, Mother Teresa began to expand the work of her Missionaries of Charity within India.

In 1959, after some of her sisters from the state of Bihar told her of the poverty there, she took a team of Missionaries of Charity 210 miles northwest of Calcutta to the city of Ranchi. This team became the first of hundreds that would go to other regions of India, neighboring countries, and, finally, continents across the seas.

During the early 1960s the Missionaries of Charity concentrated on establishing congregations throughout India. A home for the dying was constructed in Delhi, financed by unsolicited funds from supporters in Germany. In 1960 the sisters set up houses in Jhansi and Agra, two cities in the central Indian state of Uttar Pradesh. The following year Mother Teresa and the sisters established a mobile leprosy clinic in the Asansol district of Bengal. Mother Teresa was especially glad to see the opening of a house in Patna, where she had learned her medical skills.

We are not social workers but contemplatives in the world.
—MOTHER TERESA
on the Missionaries
of Charity

Impoverished Indian women hold each other as they sit on a stoop. Although many have found India's poverty overwhelming, Mother Teresa remains undaunted. "While others put questions," one associate said of her, "she solves problems."

By 1962, 119 Indian sisters had answered the call to serve the poorest of the poor with the Missionaries of Charity. Nuns were sent into 30 more centers outside Calcutta, including the Indian states of Punjab, Bihar, Maharashtra, and Kerala. In every new house, the sisters followed the daily routine established by Mother Teresa at the original house in Calcutta. The sisters arose at 4:40 A.M., put on sari and sandals, and went to chapel for prayer, meditation, and mass. They ate simple breakfasts of tea and the flat Indian bread known as *chapati*, then began their daily work with the dying, the orphans, or the lepers. After returning to the house for their main meal at noon, the sisters took a half-hour rest and then resumed their work. After prayers at chapel at 6:00 P.M., the sisters spent their evenings together, sharing observations about their

A man steers an ox-drawn cart through the streets of India's capital city, New Delhi. In the early 1960s, Mother Teresa began her drive to expand the Missionaries of Charity operations throughout India. She founded a New Delhi home for the dying in 1960.

work and stories of the people they encountered. To Mother Teresa, this spirit of community was crucial in giving the sisters the sense of family that she felt was the essence of the order. After the long, sometimes difficult days, most of the sisters were in bed by 10:00 P.M. Mother Teresa often used these late hours to work on her correspondence, responding to the many letters she received.

The Missionary of Charity congregations ranged from the snowy Himalayas in the north to the sweltering tropics of south India. Generous donations, both from wealthy Indians and from supporters in other countries, financed each new project. Many of the gifts were a result of Mother Teresa's first travels abroad. In 1960 she made a whirlwind tour of the United States. The National Council of Catholic Women invited Mother Teresa to be the speaker at their national convention in Las Vegas, Nevada. The glittering gambling and entertainment mecca was a most improbable place for such a group, but

Hindu priests (seated, foreground) invoke a rain god as followers watch the ceremony. Although the Missionaries of Charity hope that the people they help will eventually embrace the Catholic faith, they do not attempt to convert those they assist.

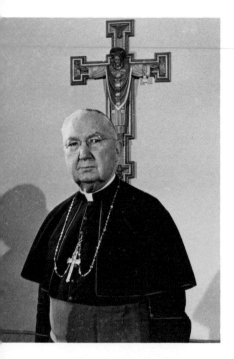

Patrick Cardinal O'Boyle, the former director of Catholic Relief Services, was impressed by Mother Teresa's devotion to India's poor. During her 1960 visit to the United States, he was one of the many clerics who donated funds to support the Missionaries of Charity.

the building, large enough to hold the gathering, had been offered free of charge. At the convention Mother Teresa spoke about her work with the poor, the ill, and the unwanted. By the conference's end, she had received hundreds of donations.

Mother Teresa then traveled to Peoria, Illinois, where she addressed a group of Catholic women who had been supporting her work since 1958. She told of an instance in which divine providence had brought together in one day all the elements necessary to open a clinic. She had received permission to use the land, the money she needed had arrived from the group in Peoria, and she had received a letter from a doctor who volunteered to run the clinic. Her ability to show people how they could aid the needy in distant countries convinced her listeners to give generously.

From Peoria, Mother Teresa went to Washington, D.C., where she met with Patrick Cardinal O'Boyle. Formerly the director of the Catholic Relief Services, he added a generous gift of money to her growing funds. Her next stop was New York and a surprise meeting with Mother Anna Dengel, the founder of the Medical Missionary Sisters, who was in New York to accept an award. Mother Teresa, always grateful for the role the Medical Missionary Sisters had played in her life, was delighted to see Mother Anna again.

Mother Teresa made several visits during her stay in New York. The staff at the headquarters office of the Catholic Relief Services welcomed her when she came to thank them for funds they had sent to India. Bishop Fulton J. Sheen called his staff together to pray with Mother Teresa when she called on him. Later that same day, she went to the United Nations and talked with a representative of the World Health Organization about the needs of the lepers in India. He gave her guidelines for getting supplies from the World Health Organization through the Indian government when she returned home.

In New York, Mother Teresa met Dorothy Day, one of the co-founders of the Catholic Worker movement. Their friendship would last until Day's death in 1980. The Catholic Worker movement, founded in 1933 with the first publication of the monthly newspaper *Catholic Worker*, was a lay program very similar to that of the Missionaries of Charity. The Catholic Workers believed in "the daily practice of the works of mercy" to the urban poor, among whom they lived. They established hospices for the sick and homeless and promoted ideas of social justice, nonviolence, and communal spirit. It was not surprising that Dorothy Day and Mother Teresa became good friends; they saw themselves as allies in God's plan.

Day took Mother Teresa on a tour through some of New York's most depressed neighborhoods. It was Mother Teresa's first encounter with men who staggered and fell not from starvation but because of alcohol and drug abuse. She was distressed at the sight of so much suffering in such an affluent nation and saddened that no one stopped to help the victims of these illnesses.

After leaving the United States, Mother Teresa journeyed to London, England, for an appearance on British television and a short visit with Mrs. Vijaya Lakshmi Pandit, India's high commissioner to the United Kingdom. Mrs. Pandit, the sister of In-

Bishop Fulton J. Sheen, an influential figure in American Catholicism, gathered his staff together to pray with Mother Teresa when she visited him in New York during her 1960 U.S. tour.

In 1933 journalist and social reformer Dorothy Day cofounded the *Catholic Worker*, a newspaper that promoted ideas of charity and social justice. Day discovered a natural ally in Mother Teresa, and the two women remained friends until Day's death in 1980.

dian prime minister Jawaharlal Nehru, was immensely pleased with Mother Teresa's work and promised to visit her in India.

Landing next in Germany, Mother Teresa was met by photographers eager to capture on film the woman responsible for Kalighat. News of her work in India had already been published in Germany in a publication called *Weltelend* (*World Misery*). A German Catholic overseas aid agency called Misereor had given Mother Teresa the funds needed to build a home for the dying in Delhi, and another organization, the Catholic Charities Agency, donated the equivalent of $25,000.

All the donors received the same sincere thanks. In *A Gift for God*, Mother Teresa explains that it is the act of giving, rather than the size of the donation, that is important: "To show great love for God and our neighbor we need not do great things. It is how much love we put in the doing that makes our offering something beautiful for God."

At last her travels led her to Rome, her final destination. In *Such a Vision of the Street*, Eileen Egan quotes Mother Teresa's letter to her sisters concerning her purpose in Rome: "I am going to try and see our Holy Father and beg of him to take our little Society under his special care and grant us a pontifical recognition." Receiving the pope's official recognition would mean that the Missionaries of Charity would answer directly to Rome and would no longer be under the authority of the archbishop of Calcutta. In order to expand their mission throughout the world, the Missionaries of Charity needed permission to obtain passports for sisters to leave India to work in other lands. The Missionaries of Charity would have to be under the jurisdiction of the Holy See to get such permission.

Before Mother Teresa left Rome, her brother, Lazar Bojaxhiu, and his family paid her a visit. Lazar, who had fought in Italy against the Nazis during World War II, had decided not to return to Albania when the communist government of Enver Hoxha took power in 1946. He now lived in Palermo with his wife, Maria, and daughter, Agi. Missing from

the family reunion, however, were Aga and Drana Bojaxhiu. Efforts to get them out of Albania, which had become a repressive communist state virtually closed to outsiders, had failed. Mother Teresa was disappointed; she had not seen her mother or sister since the day she left Skopje in 1928.

When Mother Teresa left Rome to return to the work in India, the pope had not yet decided whether to grant the Missionaries of Charity pontifical recognition. It would be almost four years before the Holy See announced its decision. Mother Teresa resolved to wait patiently; she knew India alone held enough work for a lifetime.

In 1962 the government of the Philippines became aware of Mother Teresa's efforts and awarded her the Ramon Magsaysay award. (The prize was named after the president of the Philippines, who died in 1957 in a plane crash.) She traveled to Manila to receive the award, which was given to women in Asia who worked toward peace and international understanding. The monetary gift of $6,000 allowed the Missionaries of Charity to open a children's home in Agra, India.

Albanian leader Enver Hoxha meets with villagers. Under Hoxha's repressive communist regime, established in 1946, Albanians were not allowed to leave the country. After her visit to the United States, Mother Teresa tried unsuccessfully to obtain permission for her mother and sister, who lived in the Albanian capital of Tirana, to emigrate.

Soon afterward, Mother Teresa realized it would be advantageous if a group of men began doing the same type of charitable work the sisters were engaged in. On March 25, 1963, 12 young men and a priest went to live at Shishu Bhavan to begin the studies necessary to prepare them for missionary work. According to church rules, Mother Teresa could not be the head of a male congregation, so Father Julien Henry, her longtime friend, conducted the spiritual preparation of the men who would become the Missionary Brothers of Charity.

Ian Travers-Ball, an Australian Jesuit priest ordained in 1963 as Brother Andrew, requested permission to visit the brothers for an experimental month-long stay. By the end of the month, he had shown great interest in the organization, and Mother Teresa asked him to stay on as the Missionary Brothers' director. After giving his decision a great deal of thought, he chose to break away from his first calling, just as Mother Teresa had, and left the Jesuit order to relieve Father Henry as head of the group. He adopted the title General Servant, and

Mother Teresa meets with Filipino nuns in Manila, the capital of the Philippines. In 1962 she was awarded that nation's Ramon Magsaysay award for her efforts to promote international peace and understanding.

Mother Teresa bought a simple house in Calcutta where the brothers would have their headquarters.

The Missionary Brothers of Charity went to work in areas where it was difficult for the sisters to enter. They rescued young boys from the streets and ran the men's ward at the Home for the Dying. The brothers quickly grew from a dozen volunteers to hundreds, and they eventually opened 44 houses around the world. They often entered places that Mother Teresa had deemed too dangerous for the sisters, such as Saigon, Vietnam, and the capital of Cambodia, Phnom Penh — sites ravaged by years of war. However, Mother Teresa made an effort to visit each location of the brothers, both within India and around the world.

Mother Teresa was not a timid traveler. Once she asked if she might serve as a flight attendant on an Indian airline in exchange for her ticket. Airline officials gave her a pass instead. Though she would rather have stayed at home in India than spend so many hours on airplanes, in hotels, and with the press, she knew that she could help the poor by spreading her message of urgent need. In these early years, Mother Teresa and the Missionaries of Charity could not have realized how great the benefits from her travels around the globe would become.

American soldiers in Vietnam report an air strike to headquarters in 1968. The Missionary Brothers of Charity, an all-male organization affiliated with Mother Teresa's order, traveled to dangerous regions of Vietnam and Cambodia to assist individuals who had been hurt or displaced by war.

6

"Go Ye into All the World"

In February 1965 the Missionaries of Charity learned that the Holy See had granted them pontifical recognition. Mother Teresa and the 300 women who had joined her mission could now expand their work into the rest of the world. Within five months, the sisters had set up their first center outside India, in the South American country of Venezuela.

The expansion of the Missionaries of Charity beyond India came about as a result of the Second Vatican Council, or Vatican II, an ecumenical council begun in the fall of 1962. Called by Pope John XXIII, Vatican II helped to define the role of the church in the modern world. At the council, a priest from Venezuela, Bishop Benitez, spoke with the papal internuncio (emissary) to New Delhi, Archbishop James Robert Knox, about the need for a group like the Missionaries of Charity in the poor sections of the Venezuelan countryside. Three years later, when Mother Teresa received papal permission to set up houses outside India, Bishop Benitez invited her to Venezuela. Mother Teresa personally inspected the proposed site for the new foundation and agreed to send a team of seven Indian nuns,

Calcutta was their Jerusalem, the starting point of their apostolate, which had its roots there; but the tree was to spread its branches and bear fruit in many parts of the world.
—FATHER EDWARD LE JOLY
on the expansion of the
Missionaries of Charity

Mother Teresa's Missionaries of Charity received Vatican permission to begin working around the globe in 1965. Believing that "Calcutta can be found all over the world if you have eyes to see," Mother Teresa began efforts to ease the plight of the poor throughout the world.

Simple dwellings provide shelter in the Venezuelan rain forest. In 1965 Mother Teresa founded her first mission outside India in the remote village of Cocorote, Venezuela. The sisters provided much-needed medical care and helped the local women become economically self-sufficient.

who were funded by the Diocesan Council of Catholic Women in Brooklyn, New York.

In a tiny village named Cocorote, so removed from civilization that it is not listed in any atlas, Mother Teresa and her band of sisters began their labor of love and faith. The people of Cocorote were descendants of Africans who had been brought in by Spanish colonists to work as slaves in the copper mines. They had little education and no medical facility.

In Cocorote, the needs of women and children quickly became the sisters' primary concerns. A shortage of food, clothing, and medicine was keenly felt, especially by the children. The women, encouraged to rely on men for financial support, were unable to support themselves. Social norms encouraged the men to take more than one wife with little regard to their own financial situation. If a man had taken on too large a financial burden, his whole extended family suffered. Mother Teresa's goal was to help the women of Cocorote become more self-sufficient so that they could provide for themselves and their children.

Under Mother Teresa's direction, the team of sisters cleaned up a ruined old hotel they planned to use as their headquarters. It had long been used as a dump and was infested with snakes. With the help of the townspeople, they soon had the building functioning as a center to educate and provide refuge for the women of Cocorote. The Missionaries of Charity began to teach them to sew and type. They provided elementary education to the children and taught basic English to those who expressed a desire to learn it.

The first outside missions were learning experiences for the sisters. Venezuela was very different from Calcutta; the people were from another culture, and their problems and needs had to be met in ways other than what the sisters had used in India. Mother Teresa recognized that her sisters would be going to live in unfamiliar cultures, but she never gave them specific rules to follow. The sisters at each new foundation would discover for

Sisters from the Missionaries of Charity examine a patient in a Calcutta infirmary. Although their influence began to expand across the globe in the 1960s and 1970s, the sisters never abandoned their commitment to the poor in the order's home, Calcutta.

themselves the best way to serve the people while remaining true to their vows. Mother Teresa never doubted the ability and perseverance of her sisters; she knew that they, with God's help, would find ways to give their love to the people they served.

Mother Teresa's efforts to help her own mother and sister remained unsuccessful. In 1966, after spending time in Venezuela, she went to Rome, where she tried once again to get permission for her family to leave Albania. She managed to see the Albanian attaché in Italy, who assured her his government was looking into the matter. Mother Teresa was convinced that her prayers would be answered, but Drana and Aga were never allowed out of Albania. Two years later Drana died, and Aga did not survive her for long. That she never saw her beloved mother again was a bitter disappointment to Mother Teresa, but she took joy in the fact that her mother and sister were with God.

During the 1960s and 1970s, more than 10 new

Albanian youths ride on a float adorned with the likeness of the founder of Soviet communism, Vladimir Lenin. Albania's communist government consistently thwarted Mother Teresa's efforts to get her mother and sister out, and they died without ever seeing her again.

outposts of the Missionaries of Charity were established in South America. One of the greatest joys for the sisters has been to bring the word of God to people who have only a vague notion of the Catholic church. One nun remarked, "Generally the people are baptized; but many have never seen a priest or a sister, due to the scarcity of priests and nuns. . . . So many people knew nothing about Jesus."

In 1968, three years after Mother Teresa's love for the poor invaded South America, Pope Paul VI surprised her with a request to bring a team of sisters into Rome, the center of the Catholic faith. On the outskirts of the capital of the faithful lived the very poorest people in Rome. They inhabited barrack-like buildings in an area called the *borgate*. Many had no heat, electricity, or running water and fell outside the scope of the many Catholic aid organizations already existing in the city. Once convinced that these people truly needed her help, Mother Teresa established a Missionaries of Charity organization to reach out to the destitute of Rome.

During that same year, Archbishop Perier had a discussion with the bishop of Tabora, a city in Tanzania, a country on the eastern coast of Africa. They talked about Mother Teresa and the good work done by the Missionaries of Charity. Out of that encounter Mother Teresa received an invitation to go to Tanzania in September 1968.

At the time, President Julius Nyerere was attempting to put into practice a concept called *ujamaa*, to teach the Tanzanians a system of social cooperation that would ultimately make their country self-supporting. So that certain segments of society were not marked as being in any way inferior, the word *poor* was not to be used, so Mother Teresa referred to the needy as *our people*.

The White Sisters of Africa, a long-established missionary group that took its name from the flowing white robes worn by the nuns, gave a group of buildings to the Missionaries of Charity. Though old and in need of repair, the buildings were restored and converted into an old people's home, nurseries, a medical-supply area, a kitchen, and a meeting room. Within them, abandoned children

Tanzanian president Julius Nyerere's attempt at creating an egalitarian society included the stipulation that no one in his country be labeled "poor." When the Missionaries of Charity founded centers in Tanzania, they referred to the local poor as "our people."

received care, and blind and infirm old men and women were fed and bathed.

As the Missionaries of Charity expanded their influence across the globe, Mother Teresa became aware that an increasing number of lay people wanted to be part of her organization. She wanted to give all people, including non-Catholics, the opportunity to assist the missionaries in ways that went beyond providing the nuns with donations. With the help of longtime British supporter Ann Blaikie, Mother Teresa started a group for people who wanted to help.

Ann Blaikie's association with Mother Teresa dated to the mid-1950s, when she had approached the Missionaries of Charity with suggestions for doing voluntary work. In 1960 she returned to England with her husband, John, but she kept in touch with Mother Teresa. In March 1969 Mother Teresa and Ann Blaikie formed the International Association of the Co-Workers of Mother Teresa. The organization's regulations were accepted by Pope Paul VI, and Blaikie was named chairperson. Shortly afterward her title was changed to International Link. She was only one in a long chain of people interested in doing what they could to further the work of the Missionaries of Charity.

The Co-Workers grew rapidly. Members do not have to be Catholic to join. The regulations state the two most important aspects of the group: sharing and prayer. Mother Teresa wanted the Co-Workers not only to work for the material needs of the Missionaries of Charity but also to join in the same spirit of love and compassion. The Co-Workers share their experiences to enrich each other and feel like a common family. In accordance with the organization's constitution, the Co-Workers also agree to live as simply as they can, in "voluntary poverty," with "the sacrifice of luxuries." Their meetings are held for prayer and communication; no food is served, and only water is consumed.

When many sick people wanted to become Co-Workers, Mother Teresa formed an affiliated group of Sick and Suffering Co-Workers, whose main functions are prayer and correspondence with the Mis-

We must go to those who have no one, to those who suffer from the worst disease of all, the disease of being unwanted, unloved, uncared for.
—MOTHER TERESA
in a message to her
Co-Workers

sionaries of Charity. Mother Teresa holds a unique outlook on suffering. She feels that the sick experience more of Jesus's sufferings on a daily basis than healthy people do and therefore have greater empathy in prayer for the world's suffering.

Mother Teresa once told Jacqueline de Decker, a Belgian woman who was the link for the Sick and Suffering Co-Workers, "Our Lord must love you much to give you so great a part in his suffering." De Decker, whose sole desire had been to become a missionary, was stricken by paralysis and underwent a series of 20 operations on her spine. She located other terminally ill or disabled people who wanted to help Mother Teresa with their prayers. By 1985 the Sick and Suffering Co-Workers boasted a membership of 2,600. For Mother Teresa, every one of them had a role to play. It did not matter that their bodies were unable to function as healthy ones; their suffering and prayers were help enough to her. She told them, "The work [in the slums] is tremendous and I need workers, it is true, but I need souls like yours to pray and suffer for the work."

The accomplishments of the Missionaries of Charity did not go unnoticed by the religious world. In 1971 Mother Teresa received the first Pope John XXIII Peace Prize from Pope Paul VI. He awarded it

Mother Teresa, seated behind Pope Paul VI, is honored at a 1971 Vatican ceremony. Mother Teresa received the Pope John XXIII Peace Prize — one of the first of many such honors — which not only drew attention to the work of the Missionaries of Charity, but added $67,000 to their budget to aid the poor.

to her on Epiphany, a Christian festival celebrating Jesus's birth. He commended her for her work with the poor, her Christian love, and her efforts for peace. Along with a small statue of Christ, he presented her with 50 million Italian lire (about $67,000).

September 1969 saw Mother Teresa and the Missionaries of Charity in a completely different part of the world — Australia. Archbishop Knox had often spoken to Mother Teresa about his native Australia. An avid opponent of racism, his concern was for the aborigines, a dark-skinned people who had inhabited the continent for thousands of years before white settlers arrived, pushing the aborigines off their land and turning them into an oppressed minority. Knox asked Mother Teresa to go to Australia and do what she could for them.

Mother Teresa accepted his invitation, and sent a team to New South Wales, in southeastern Australia. With her special wisdom, she chose sisters from a shorter, darker-skinned Indian tribe in Ranchi, India, so that the missionaries might be more readily accepted by the aborigines. Indeed, like many of the aborigines, some of these sisters stood less than five feet tall.

Mother Teresa not only supervised the beginning of this work, but as in every case, she worked diligently along with her sisters when she first visited the living quarters of the aborigines. The sisters began regular visits to poor families to administer medication, advice, comfort, and companionship. They also raised funds for a bus to transport aboriginal children to and from school. In *A Gift For God*, Mother Teresa describes a visit with an old aboriginal man as she cleaned his room: "There was in that room a beautiful lamp, covered for many years with dirt. I asked him: 'Why do you not light the lamp?' 'For whom?' he said. . . . I asked him: 'Will you light the lamp if a Sister comes to see you?' He said: 'Yes, if I hear a human voice, I will do it.' The other day he sent me word: 'Tell my friend that the light she has lighted in my life is still burning.' "

Mother Teresa and her sisters brought their ser-

vices to other developed countries. When Mother Teresa had journeyed through the New York borough of the Bronx during her 1960 trip to America, she had become aware of its poverty and decay. The Missionaries of Charity set up a convent in a poor, crime-ridden section of the South Bronx in 1971. As Mother Teresa reports, "The Sisters are doing small things in New York, helping the children, visiting the lonely, the sick, the unwanted. We know now that being unwanted is the greatest disease of all. That is the poverty we find around us here." She felt that poverty in the Bronx was deeper even than in Calcutta because often the poor went completely unnoticed. An elderly person, afraid or unable to go out, might die alone and not be missed for days. To remedy this situation, teams of sisters went into the tenements to visit the shut-ins, clean houses, bring groceries, and simply to listen.

The welfare of the young people of the Bronx was of great concern to Mother Teresa and the sisters.

Two boys play on an abandoned car in the South Bronx. When Mother Teresa's nuns set up a mission in the impoverished New York City neighborhood in 1971, they hoped to break the cycle of poverty by educating the area's children and building their self-esteem.

In order to keep the children off the streets, her sisters initiated a camp program of art and sports activities similar to those found at expensive camps in rural areas. They held the free programs each day on the grounds of a school in the Bronx, offering the children classes in crafts, drama, sports, reading, and music.

The mission in the South Bronx was only the beginning of the Missionaries of Charity's work in the United States. In San Francisco, California, a large, well-furnished building donated to the organization was felt by Mother Teresa to be rather big and too elegant. She and her team got rid of everything they did not need, from the pews in the chapel to the rugs and mattresses. They even turned down an offer to fix the hot-water tank in the basement.

Many people do not understand why anyone would want to do without the comforts most people take for granted, but Mother Teresa believes that all who would help the poor must experience poverty.

A Bronx woman presses her cheek to Mother Teresa's hand in a gesture of gratitude. The Missionaries of Charity have been very active in New York, assisting the poor, visiting shut-ins, and caring for the victims of acquired immune deficiency syndrome (AIDS).

She has always been uncomfortable with organized fund-raising activities, remarking, "I don't want the work to become a business but to remain a work of love." She and the Missionaries of Charity have been able to rely on goodwill to support their work. According to Mother Teresa, "There has not been one single day that we have refused somebody, that we did not have a bed or something, and we deal with thousands of people."

In *The Love of Christ*, edited by Georges Gorree and Jean Barbier, Mother Teresa's thoughts on the vows of poverty taken by the order are recorded. "Our strict poverty is our safeguard. We do not want to begin by serving the poor and little by little end up serving the rich, like other religious orders in history. In order to understand and help those who lack everything, we must live like them. The difference is that our destitute ones are poor by force of circumstance, whereas we are by choice."

October 1971 brought another honor to Mother Teresa when the politically prominent Kennedy family gave her the Joseph P. Kennedy Foundation Award. Senator Edward Kennedy presented her with a check for $12,000. He praised her ability to recognize human needs and her unshakable faith that God would provide what the sisters needed. The money was immediately earmarked for disabled and retarded children, who would be provided with a new home in India: the Nirmala Kennedy Center.

These had been busy, productive, lifesaving years spent by Mother Teresa and the Missionaries of Charity, obeying the Bible's command "Go ye into all the world and preach the gospel." Perhaps the aging and somewhat frail woman would now start to slow down. But Mother Teresa was far from content with sitting back while there was still so much more to be done.

Mother Teresa has personally succeeded in bridging the gulf that exists between the rich nations and the poor nations. Her view of the dignity of man has built a bridge.
—KATHRYN SPINK
British author

7

World Traveler

In 1971 Mother Teresa turned 61, an age when most people begin to think of retiring or at least slowing down. Mother Teresa, however, continued her hectic schedule and traveled to war-torn Bangladesh. This tiny country, about the size of the state of Wisconsin, holds the ninth-largest population in the world. It was the eastern part of Pakistan until 1971, when civil war erupted after East Pakistan declared its independence. West Pakistani troops moved in, killing more than 3 million people.

By 1972, Bangladesh, as it was renamed after winning independence, was being referred to as an "international basket case." Crowded to the limit with refugees from the political conflict, the country was the scene of horrible devastation. Villages had been leveled in the fighting, and food was scarce. Thousands were starving. On top of the anguish, more than 200,000 women had been raped by the occupying armies. Muslim law dictated that these victims be treated as outcasts and abandoned by their families. In desperation, many of these women committed suicide.

In response to the crisis in Bangladesh, Mother Teresa and the Missionaries of Charity arrived as part of one of the first international convoys into the suffering nation. She and her sisters went right

Mother Teresa is possessed by a burning desire for a universal presence and action. In this she mirrors St. Paul, who traveled from one place to another . . . craving to go to the extremities of the world to preach Christ.
—FATHER EDWARD LE JOLY
adviser to the Missionaries of Charity

Refugees line up at a Missionaries of Charity aid station. In 1972 Mother Teresa took the sisters into Bangladesh, which had recently declared its independence from Pakistan and provoked a bloody civil war. The sisters provided food and medical supplies and protected local women from marauding soldiers.

to work burying the dead, tending to the wounded, comforting those they could, and hiding many young women from marauding soldiers. Mother Teresa began to arrange for the adoptions of the unwanted babies, and offers came in from several countries in Europe. She hoped that these acts of kindness would, in some small way, disrupt the cycle of bitterness and hatred that threatened to engulf the nation. Eventually, the Missionaries of Charity expanded their work in Bangladesh and established four centers there, backing their words of love with practical, hard work.

Mother Teresa's efforts in Bangladesh and around the world earned her India's Nehru Award in 1972. When Indian president V. V. Giri presented the award, he called Mother Teresa an "emancipated soul who has transcended all barriers of race, religion, creed, and nation." He went on to say, "In an embittered world of many wars and hatred, the life and work of Mother Teresa bring new hope for the future of mankind."

One area that seemed perpetually doomed to the "embittered world of many wars and hatred" was the Middle East. By 1970, the year the Missionaries of Charity established their first house in this troubled region, the Middle East had seen three major wars, and there was constant friction between Israel and its Arab neighbors, who did not recognize the Jewish state as legitimate. In July 1970 five sisters from the Missionaries of Charity settled in Amman, Jordan, to help the many refugees who had crowded into the capital city after the Six-Day War of 1967. In that conflict, the Israelis had captured and occupied the West Bank of the Jordan River, and thousands of Palestinians had fled into neighboring Jordan, putting a severe strain on the nation's economy. Worried by the volatile political atmosphere of the time, Mother Teresa remained with her sisters in Amman for six weeks. Shortly after she left Jordan, a civil war erupted. After calm was restored, the sisters tended to the wounded and the homeless.

The 1967 war had also resulted in the creation of hundreds of thousands of refugees in the Gaza

> To meet her is to feel utterly humble, to sense the power of tenderness and the strength of love.
>
> —INDIRA GANDHI
> prime minister of India
> (1966–77, 1980–84), on
> Mother Teresa

Strip, a slice of land at the northeast corner of the Sinai Peninsula, between Israel and Egypt. Mother Teresa and the Missionaries of Charity began their work in Gaza in 1973, the year of the bloody Yom Kippur War. The compound they took over had recently been evacuated after the murder of the Catholic priest who worked there, but that news did not deter Mother Teresa. She and a team of young Indian nuns quickly set up a mission to aid some of the 380,000 Arabs who had fled into Gaza during the years of fighting. These displaced people had lost their land and their homes. The sisters provided shelter, health care, and education for the children.

At the other end of the Arabian peninsula, in the tiny Muslim nation of Yemen, the government had built a large hospital, but it could not be staffed because of a lack of trained workers. Officials there invited Mother Teresa and the sisters to staff the hospital. Unfortunately, one of the rules of the Missionaries of Charity stated that the nuns could not staff an institution. Gracious even in refusal, Mother Teresa said they would be willing to go to

Machine gun at the ready, an Israeli soldier watches a crowd in the city of Bethlehem on the Israeli-occupied West Bank of Jordan. The Missionaries of Charity opened their first house in the Middle East in 1970.

Yemen if there were poor who could be helped. The prime minister issued a formal invitation, and the necessary groundwork of finding a building, bringing in a priest, and organizing a team was completed. The work began officially on August 22, 1973. When Yemen's government presented Mother Teresa with a "sword of honor" as a gesture of appreciation, she good-naturedly laughed about it afterward. "A sword, to me!" she exclaimed.

The team established a clinic, a home for the destitute, and Dar Al-Salem, an asylum for the mentally ill. They did not preach their faith but rather lived out their convictions within the strictures of Yemen's Muslim culture. According to Mother Teresa, the Missionaries of Charity are less interested in increasing the Catholic fold than in guiding people to become the best they can be within their own religions.

It was an amazing accomplishment for a Catholic nun and her teams of sisters to be invited into Muslim countries. Several more locations in the Middle East were targeted by the Missionaries of Charity,

Sister and brother hold hands in the barren countryside around Taiz, North Yemen. Yemen is one of the many Muslim countries where the Missionaries of Charity have worked within the strictures of local religious beliefs.

including Cairo, Egypt, where they worked among the garbage pickers: men, women, and children who earned their living by collecting, sifting through, and selling other people's refuse. The poorest of the poor in Cairo, they lived at the garbage dumps.

The world was beginning to watch Mother Teresa. She disliked publicity about herself but did not refuse the opportunity to appear at meetings or accept awards if it meant she could tell the world about the Missionaries of Charity and the work they did. Despite her simplicity, Mother Teresa was not naive about the impact media attention could have on her work. She wanted to reach as many people as possible with reports on the goodness of the poor and the need to care for them. Articles about her and the Missionaries of Charity began to appear on a fairly regular basis in publications around the world. The British Broadcasting Corporation interviewed her, and the editor of England's *Punch* magazine, Malcolm Muggeridge, made a film about her work, *Something Beautiful for God*. His introduction to Mother Teresa made a profound impression on Muggeridge, who described his subject as "a burning and shining light" and "a living embodiment of Christ's gospel of love."

In 1973 Mother Teresa received the Templeton Prize for Progress in Religion, sponsored by Mr. and Mrs. John Templeton, a prominent English couple. The Templetons used their personal fortune to further understanding in religion. The judges had to decide on 1 person out of 2,000 nominations. One Hindu, one Muslim, one Jew, one Buddhist, and three others representing various Christian groups sat down together and chose Mother Teresa because "she has been instrumental in widening and deepening man's knowledge and love of God, and thereby furthering the quest for the quality of life that mirrors the Divine."

During the next year, Mother Teresa and the Missionaries of Charity established two houses in Papua New Guinea. The biggest challenge they faced in this South Pacific nation was communication. On the relatively small land area, there were 700

Britain's prince Philip congratulates Mother Teresa on her receipt of the Templeton Prize for Progress in Religion. She was given the award in 1973 for "deepening man's knowledge and love of God."

A beaming Mother Teresa attends the World Conference of the International Women's Year in Mexico City, Mexico. Representing the Vatican, she drew the other delegates' attention to the hardships of poor women throughout the world.

languages spoken. Often people from one village could not speak the language of their closest neighbors. The sisters, as they did wherever they went, diligently began to study the local languages and set forth to seek out and minister to the poor. They would not let language barriers stand in their way, and eventually two more houses were organized in Papua New Guinea.

By the mid-1970s, Mother Teresa had become a familiar face as a world traveler. In 1975 the Vatican asked her to attend the World Conference of the International Women's Year in Mexico City. As a member of the Vatican delegation, Mother Teresa presented the papal contribution, entitled "Women in Poverty," which urged "all women to have a special concern for poor and disadvantaged women on whom poverty places particularly crushing burdens." During the conference breaks, Mother Teresa visited the poor of the city. News of her activities reached Mexico's president, Luis Echeverría Álvarez, who asked to meet Mother Teresa and invited her to set up houses in Mexico.

Within the year, the Missionaries of Charity had moved in to assist the poor of Mexico City. Like the garbage pickers in Cairo, many of these people lived at the enormous city dump, staying alive by sorting through refuse and selling usable trash. With the help of President Echeverría, Mother Teresa and her sisters established a home for the destitute, a clinic, a children's home, and a convent for the Missionaries of Charity. Over the next several years, missions opened in five other nations: Guatemala, Haiti, Panama, the Dominican Republic, and Honduras.

Not all of the congregations set up by the Missionaries of Charity were success stories. Despite an invitation to open a house in Sri Lanka, a country that usually rejected all religious orders, the Missionaries of Charity eventually were asked to leave. A more spectacular failure occurred in Belfast, Ire-

Mother Teresa befriends a group of children in Belfast, Northern Ireland. The Missionaries of Charity opened a Belfast mission in 1972 but left after their plea for interreligious toleration was ignored by both the Protestant majority and the Catholic minority.

land, a region torn by religious and political differences. There, hatred of the minority Catholics thundered from the Protestant pulpits of such fire-eaters as Reverend Ian Paisley, and desperate Catholics turned to the terrorist solutions of the Irish Republican Army. Mother Teresa and four Indian sisters went to Belfast in 1972 to bring a desperately needed message of sharing and unity, only to be ignored by both sides. The sisters soon left the unhappy land.

As happens with most every organization, some members of the Missionaries became disillusioned and left the society. In *Servant of Love*, author Edward Le Joly lists a number of such cases. At one house, the mother superior ran off with the local parish priest, the spiritual director of the convent. One sister married the leper she had been treating; another left the order to marry a co-worker she had come to know. Mother Teresa is always saddened at the loss of a sister or brother who leaves the organization. She cannot comprehend reneging on what she considers a pledge made to God, but she understands that people make mistakes, and she accepts it as God's will. "We remain very human; we have our ups and downs," she admits.

In Peru the sisters were confronted by a group of priests who told them to leave because, the priests felt, the sisters were only perpetuating the cycle of poverty, not addressing its underlying causes. Critics have leveled this particular charge against Mother Teresa and the Missionaries of Charity many times, saying that the work done by the Missionaries of Charity is only a bandage, not a cure.

Mother Teresa, who maintains a detachment from political action, comes under criticism because her ambition is not to alter conditions through political channels but to comfort those who already suffer. In a 1982 interview with Beverly Beyette of the *Los Angeles Times*, Mother Teresa responded, "I'm not trying to change anything. Somebody said to me, 'Why do you give them the fish to eat? Why don't you give them the rope to catch the fish?' " Mother Teresa went on to explain that the poor

I suppose the simplest explanation for the great popularity of Mother Teresa is that, in a world of structures and technology in which no person seems to matter very much, she has affirmed the preciousness of each human life.

—ABIGAIL MCCARTHY
American author
and columnist

Shielded from the Florida sun by an umbrella, Mother Teresa addresses reporters at a 1981 Miami press conference. She announced the opening of a Missionaries of Charity shelter for impoverished women.

scraps of humanity the Missionaries of Charity reach are far too disabled and needy to "learn to fish." They can barely stand, much less hold a net. Mother Teresa contends that when the poor are strong enough to leave her, there will be someone to teach them to fish. Her detractors argue that this fatalistic view is not mirrored in reality and does nothing to educate the poor to help them break out of the circle of poverty.

When Mother Teresa began her order in Calcutta, she told a friend that "good works are a link forming a chain of love around the world." Despite the occasional setback and the sometimes harsh criticism, with the establishment of each new mission the chain has grown stronger.

8

Serving the Prince of Peace

It would take several books to tell about the establishment of all the houses of the Missionaries of Charity and Mother Teresa's involvement in each one. Mother Teresa has never turned down an invitation to work among the poorest of the poor on any continent. The Missionaries of Charity, along with the Missionary Brothers of Charity, have brought care and love to thousands of people because one woman saw the need and said, "I will."

By 1976, 25 years had passed since Mother Teresa began her work in Calcutta. She had freely devoted her life to serve the world's destitute, and thousands had joined her in her work. In honor of that silver anniversary, Mother Teresa sent out invitations in the form of requests to every religious organization in Calcutta. She requested not a party or gifts but that each group hold a thanksgiving service of its own to thank God for the blessings bestowed on the work of the Missionaries of Charity.

As she had hoped, the celebrations turned out to be simple. She had requested "No expenses, no concerts, no decorations, only 'Thank you God.' I want God to be the central figure in our celebration so

At times, I feel rather sad, because we do so little. Most people praise us for our actions, but what we do is not more than a drop of water in the ocean. It hardly affects the immensity of human suffering.
—MOTHER TERESA

Standing in front of a Calcutta shrine to the Virgin Mary, Mother Teresa contemplates the immense tasks that remain ahead. Believing that "good works are a link forming a chain of love around the world," she has pledged to offer assistance and hope wherever she and her sisters are needed.

that everybody's attention may be drawn to God and all may acknowledge that it is his work and not ours." Catholics, Jews, Protestants, Orthodox Christians, Muslims, Methodists, Jains, Hindus, Parsis, Buddhists, and others joined in with Mother Teresa and the Missionaries of Charity to thank God for the 25 years of their association with the poor.

The Silver Jubilee was celebrated during the week of September 28, 1976. Each day, a service of thanksgiving was held in a place of worship. Eighteen different religious groups participated, each in its own way. After reciting their own prayers, 5,000 Muslims said a prayer of thanks for the sisters and their work. A Hindu *puja*, or prayer, was offered in the Temple of Shree Lakshmi Narayan, the holy men calling on the thousand names of God in Sanskrit. Mother Teresa attended a prayer meeting at a Sikh temple. Catholic priests prayed for a long life for Mother Teresa and asked God's blessings on the Missionaries of Charity.

On October 7, Michael Gomes, the layman who had first housed Mother Teresa, helped Father Celeste Van Exem and Archbishop Picachy of Calcutta

An Indian Catholic displays a portrait of Jesus Christ. In 1976 Mother Teresa celebrated 25 years of work by the Missionaries of Charity with a week-long thanksgiving service.

celebrate mass. Nuns from all over Calcutta came to the organization's headquarters on Lower Circular Road to give thanks for Mother Teresa and the Missionaries of Charity.

Looking forward to another 25 years, Mother Teresa began 1977 with increased vigor. The next decade saw the creation of about 100 new missions, bringing the total to 350 houses at the end of 1986. By that time, more than 2,500 young women had cut their hair as a sign of obedience and joined the Missionaries of Charity. Together with the men who joined the Missionary Brothers, they labored all over the world, giving aid, comfort, and love wherever Mother Teresa saw that they were needed.

Mother Teresa received several more awards during this decade. England's Cambridge University conferred upon her an honorary doctor of divinity degree. In 1979 the president of Italy, Sandro Pertini, presented her with the Balzan International Prize. Financed by the will of a wealthy Italian humanitarian named Angela Balzan Danieli, the award was given to Mother Teresa for her efforts toward peace and brotherhood and added $325,000 to the budget of the Missionaries of Charity. As always, the monies awarded to Mother Teresa went directly to aiding the poor.

Mother Teresa herself remained indifferent to the honorary degrees and the mountains of praise lavished upon her. She made the appearances and gave the speeches because she felt that "it is Christ using me as his instrument to unite up all the people present. . . . I feel that to bring all these people together to talk about God is really wonderful. A new hope for the world."

Mother Teresa was yet to win one prize that would outshine all the others as a recognition of her contribution to humanity. In February 1979 the Nobel Prize committee began to sift through the 50 nominations for that year's recipient of the peace prize. To win a Nobel award is always a great honor, but the prize for peace has held a place of highest esteem as the grandest and most difficult award to attain. Presented yearly since 1901, the Nobel Peace Prize

> *I am myself unworthy of the prize. I do not want it personally. But by this award the Norwegian people have recognized the existence of the poor. It is on their behalf that I have come.*
> —MOTHER TERESA
> on accepting the Nobel
> Peace Prize

Mother Teresa leaves an Oslo church after attending services. She came to the Norwegian capital in December 1979 to receive the Nobel Peace Prize. Perhaps the world's greatest honor, the prize has also been awarded to such luminaries as medical missionary Albert Schweitzer and civil rights leader Martin Luther King, Jr.

has been awarded to such outstanding servants of peace as Jean Henri Dunant, the Swiss founder of the International Red Cross; Albert Schweitzer, the Alsatian theologian and medical missionary who established a hospital in Gabon, Africa; and Martin Luther King, Jr., the American civil rights leader who strove for racial equality and interracial understanding in the United States.

Mother Teresa was not a new name to the Nobel committee. In 1972 former prime minister of Canada Lester Pearson had submitted Mother Teresa's name for the peace prize. Three years later Robert S. McNamara, the president of the World Bank, had again suggested Mother Teresa, and it was his original 1975 proposal that was resubmitted in 1979. Because the World Bank dealt with the problems of developing nations, McNamara was familiar with Mother Teresa's work in India. In his proposal, he wrote that she deserved the peace prize because "she advances peace in the most fundamental way possible: by her extraordinary reaffirmation of the inviolability of human dignity." He then explained the most compelling reason for proposing Mother Teresa for the award: "But more important than the organizational structure of her work is the message it conveys; that genuine peace is not the mere absence of hostilities, but rather the tranquility that arises out of a social order in which individuals treat one another with justice and compassion." In October 1979 the final decision was announced: Mother Teresa had won the Nobel Peace Prize. Word was sent to her in India, and the news traveled quickly throughout the world, elating her friends and supporters.

On December 9, 1979, an awe-inspiring sight greeted Mother Teresa as she disembarked at the airport in Oslo, Norway, where she had flown to accept the award. Thousands of cheering followers stood in the freezing weather, each holding a lighted candle. Dressed as always, in her simple sari and sandals, the diminutive nun greeted the crowd of well-wishers.

Later that evening, in the huge hall of Oslo University, the Nobel ceremony began. Soft lights made the white marble walls and pillars gleam; seven magnificent bouquets of orange, yellow, and white chrysanthemums and gladiolus decorated the stage. A 50-piece orchestra played *Gratitude* by Norwegian composer Edvard Grieg as Mother Teresa was led to the stage. Professor John Sannes, chairman of the Norwegian Nobel Committee, presented Mother Teresa with the Nobel Peace Prize and a check for $190,000. He stressed her dedication to the poor and her love for humanity and, quoting from McNamara's letter, emphasized her manner of promoting peace and alleviating suffering by restoring human dignity.

As the applause of the audience died down, Mother Teresa began to speak. Her sun-browned face, creased with lines, reflected the pain, suffer-

Mother Teresa displays the Nobel Peace Prize following the award ceremony in Oslo. "People must love one another," she stated in her heartfelt acceptance speech, "so no one feels unwanted, especially the children."

ing, hardship, and joy she had experienced during her years of missionary work. She spoke, without notes, for 30 minutes.

"People must love one another," she insisted, "So no one feels unwanted, especially the children." In 1979, designated the Year of the Child by the United Nations, Mother Teresa made an impassioned speech against abortion. In Norway, where government funding is available to women who choose to terminate their pregnancies, Mother Teresa's words were a challenge: "[Abortion] is the greatest destroyer of peace today. Because if a mother can kill her own child — what is left but for me to kill you and you to kill me — there is nothing in between. . . . Let us bring back the child, and this year being the child's year!"

She went on to speak of God's good news: "The news was peace to all of goodwill and this is something we all want — the peace of the heart." She told of being with a destitute woman when she died. The woman did not complain of her miserable life or bemoan her fate, but rather, recounted Mother Teresa, "She took hold of my hand, as she said one word only, 'Thank you' — and she died." After pausing, she added, "The poor are very wonderful people."

After telling a few more of her stories of work among the poor, she asked for prayers for the Missionaries of Charity and her co-workers around the world. Nearing the end of her speech, she encouraged everyone to love one another as Jesus did and to share his love with all. In conclusion, her face radiant with joy, she said, "God bless you!" and returned to her seat. The audience responded with thunderous applause.

Throughout all the glitter, ceremony, and applause, Mother Teresa retained her humility. Accepting nothing but water at the reception after the ceremony, she greeted almost 1,000 guests. For the first time in the history of the Nobel Prize, the traditional banquet had been canceled at the request of the recipient. The $6,000 projected dinner expense was given to Mother Teresa for the poor.

A day filled with public appearances and interviews followed, but after a brief visit with her brother Lazar and his daughter, Agi, Mother Teresa was on her way to Rome to attend a mass celebrated by Pope John Paul II. She brought several of her sisters into his private chapel, where they sat on the floor to listen to him. She warmed to his simplicity and humility. He seemed like a real father to her.

Three months after the Nobel Prize ceremony, her adopted country of India awarded her its highest civilian honor, the *Bharat Ratna* — the Jewel of India. Mother Teresa was the first naturalized Indian citizen to receive this prestigious award. Biographer Egan writes that Indian president Neelam Sanjiva

Mother Teresa and Pope John Paul II greet a welcoming crowd on a tour of one of the Calcutta missions. After receiving the Nobel Prize, Mother Teresa went to Rome to attend a mass given by the pope in his private chapel.

First Lady Nancy Reagan looks on as U.S. president Ronald Reagan presents Mother Teresa with the Presidential Medal of Freedom in 1985. Commending her on her work in the United States and around the world, he characterized her as "a heroine of our time."

Reddy, who presented the award, told the audience, "Mother Teresa embodies in herself compassion and love of humanity as few in history have done. . . ." Prime Minister Indira Gandhi, who strongly disagreed with Mother Teresa's Catholic stance on family planning and birth control in India, was present to congratulate her.

Mother Teresa continued to visit the United States on a regular basis. In fact, Americans have entered into both ends of Mother Teresa's world — as both givers and receivers. By 1984 the Missionaries of Charity had established 19 houses to help the American poor and homeless. In addition, there are hundreds of co-workers. Many U.S. agencies, such as Food for Peace, CARE, Church World Service, and Catholic Relief Services, regularly supply food for Mother Teresa's organizations around the world. In 1985 President Ronald Reagan awarded Mother Teresa the Presidential Medal of Freedom. That same year, when the United Nations celebrated its 40th anniversary, more than 1,000 diplomats and dignitaries from around the world assembled in the great vaulted hall of the UN General Assembly in New York to listen to Mother Teresa speak of poverty and compassion and Christ's love. Although Mother Teresa said nothing new, nothing she had not been saying for the past 30 years, the audience leaned forward eagerly to catch every word from the slightly stooped, elderly woman wearing the trademark blue-bordered sari and sandals.

Despite her advanced years, Mother Teresa has continued to travel extensively. Visiting the houses for the poor that the Missionaries of Charity have established in 70 countries helps her maintain contact with her sisters. Speaking engagements, educational efforts, and her ongoing work with the poor keep her far busier than she ever dreamed possible. Although the number of suffering people in the world remains staggering, she continues, undaunted. "I never add up," she has said. "I only subtract from the total dying. . . . It is not the magnitude of our actions but the amount of love that is put into them that matters."

In 1985 Mother Teresa even made a rare visit to the communist People's Republic of China, where she met with Deng Pufang, the handicapped son of China's leader Deng Xiaoping. Mother Teresa commended the young man, who championed the cause of China's millions of handicapped, but never afraid to say what she believes, she declared that no matter what Deng Pufang said, he was not truly an atheist. (Communists reject all religion.) "The same loving hand created you and me," she responded to Deng's assertion of his atheism. "In your heart you have a desire to love God. You put that desire into action and that is love."

Mother Teresa believes that each suffering person is "Jesus in a distressing disguise." In 1987 this conviction compelled her to reach out to men and women suffering from the ravages of the recently discovered acquired immune deficiency syndrome (AIDS), a disease that destroys the body's immune

Mother Teresa takes her leave of Deng Pufang, son of Chinese premier Deng Xiaoping. During her 1985 visit to the People's Republic of China, she applauded the young man's work to aid the handicapped even as she criticized the atheist philosophy espoused by the Chinese Communist party.

system, making the victim susceptible to all kinds of deadly infection. Like the lepers Mother Teresa worked with in India, AIDS sufferers are the victims not only of disease but of ignorance. Many people who have not learned about how the disease is transmitted shun those with AIDS because they fear that they, too, may catch it. Thus, for many victims, the agony of knowing that they have a fatal disease is compounded by a desperate loneliness. To help AIDS sufferers spend their last days in a supportive, loving environment, Mother Teresa opened hospices in New York and California. She appealed to prison authorities on behalf of AIDS-stricken patients, and as a result of her efforts, they were granted medical furloughs in order to be transferred to a hospice where they could receive appropriate care and die in peace. Fittingly, the men were released on Christmas Eve.

Whether in Kalighat, looking into the eyes of a dying Hindu, or receiving a standing ovation in the UN General Assembly, Mother Teresa remains unafraid to reach out and love, always ready to counter

Mother Teresa greets a boy outside a San Francisco, California, church in 1986. She had just accepted the vows of 10 new Missionaries of Charity sisters. Her organization has grown to include thousands of nuns worldwide.

Mother Teresa kneels in prayer. Guided by the conviction that she is serving God by ministering to the ailing, destitute, and helpless, Mother Teresa has had a tremendous impact not only on those she has helped directly, but also on people who have been touched by her example of love in action.

despair with hope. She is considered by many an open channel from God to the world. Even those who disagree with her methods or do not share her religious beliefs acknowledge that she is an extraordinary individual.

A simple woman of humble origins, she has saved thousands of lives and touched millions more. Fueled by faith in God and respect for humanity, she has made a vast difference in the world. Mother Teresa has never led a nation or commanded an army, but she is a world leader nonetheless. She and her followers have marshaled the forces of compassion to alleviate suffering, restore self-respect, and impart hope.

Day by day Mother Teresa and her sisters and brothers continue to do small things with great love: "It isn't how much we do, but how much love we put into doing it. Not how much we give, but how much love we put into giving. To God there is nothing small. The moment we give it to God it becomes infinite."

Further Reading

Egan, Eileen. *Such a Vision of the Street*. New York: Doubleday, 1985.

Le Joly, Edward. *Mother Teresa of Calcutta*. San Francisco: Harper & Row, 1977.

Muggeridge, Malcolm. *Something Beautiful for God*. New York: Image Books, 1977.

Porter, David. *Mother Teresa: The Early Years*. Grand Rapids, MI: William B. Eerdmans Publishing Company, 1986.

Serrou, Robert. *Teresa of Calcutta*. New York: McGraw-Hill, 1981.

Spink, Kathryn. *The Miracle of Love*. San Francisco: Harper & Row, 1981.

Chronology

Aug. 27, 1910	Born Agnes Gonxha Bojaxhiu to an Albanian merchant family in Skopje, Macedonia
Sept. 25, 1928	Leaves Skopje to join Loreto order in Dublin, Ireland
Jan. 1929	Arrives in Calcutta, India, to begin missionary work
May 1931	Takes first vows, adopts name Teresa; begins teaching at Loreto Entally convent school
May 14, 1937	Takes final vows
Aug. 16, 1948	Leaves Loreto order to begin work with the poor in the slums of Calcutta
Dec. 1948	Opens her first school for slum children
1949	Granted Indian citizenship
Oct. 7, 1950	Becomes mother superior of her own order, the Missionaries of Charity
1953	Missionaries of Charity official headquarters established in Calcutta
1954	Mother Teresa founds *Nirmal Hriday*, the Home for the Dying, first of the Missionaries of Charity establishments in Calcutta
1959	Begins to expand order within India
March 25, 1963	Missionary Brothers of Charity established
Feb. 1965	Missionaries of Charity receive pontifical recognition; begin expansion outside India
March 1969	International Association of Co-Workers of Mother Teresa founded, allowing lay persons
Jan. 6, 1971	Mother Teresa is awarded Pope John XXIII Peace Prize
Sept. 1976	Celebrates Silver Jubilee of Missionaries of Charity with interdenominational prayers
Dec. 10, 1979	Receives Nobel Peace Prize
March 1980	Awarded the Jewel of India, her adopted country's highest civilian honor
1985	Receives Presidential Medal of Honor from U.S. president Ronald Reagan
	Visits communist People's Republic of China
1987	Attends to the needs of AIDS victims

Index

Joan Graff Clucas, a graduate of Biola University, lives in Upland, California, with her husband and three children. She has taught elementary school since 1964 and is presently teaching fifth grade at Carnelian Elementary School in Alta Loma.

Arthur M. Schlesinger, jr., taught history at Harvard for many years and is currently Albert Schweitzer Professor of the Humanities at City University of New York. He is the author of numerous highly praised works in American history and has twice been awarded the Pulitzer Prize. He served in the White House as special assistant to Presidents Kennedy and Johnson.

PICTURE CREDITS

AP/Wide World Photos: pp. 14, 15, 44, 59, 61, 68, 72, 81, 89, 90, 91, 93, 95, 100, 105, 106; Culver Pictures: pp. 20, 21, 24, 28, 36; Eastfoto: pp. 18, 23, 71, 78; Mark Godfrey/Archive Pictures, Inc.: p. 86; Abigail Heyman/Archive Pictures, Inc.: pp. 32, 58; Paolo Koch/Photo Researchers, Inc.: p. 30; Betty Lane/Photo Researchers, Inc.: p. 92; Mary Ellen Mark/Archive Pictures, Inc.: pp. 2, 40, 47, 48, 50, 52, 55, 57, 63, 64, 77, 98; Photo Researchers, Inc.: p. 76; Reuters/Bettmann Newsphotos: p. 103; From *Such a Vision of the Street: Mother Teresa—The Spirit and the Work*, Eileen Egan, 1985, Doubleday. Used by permission of the publisher: pp. 25, 29, 31, 37; Sygma: pp. 12, 26, 41, 62, 66, 74, 83, 84, 96, 101; UPI/Bettmann Newsphotos: pp. 17, 33, 34, 38, 43, 45, 49, 56, 67, 69, 70, 73, 79, 104, 107